S0-BBI-202

JERICHO

THE HISTORY OF A
LONG ISLAND HAMLET

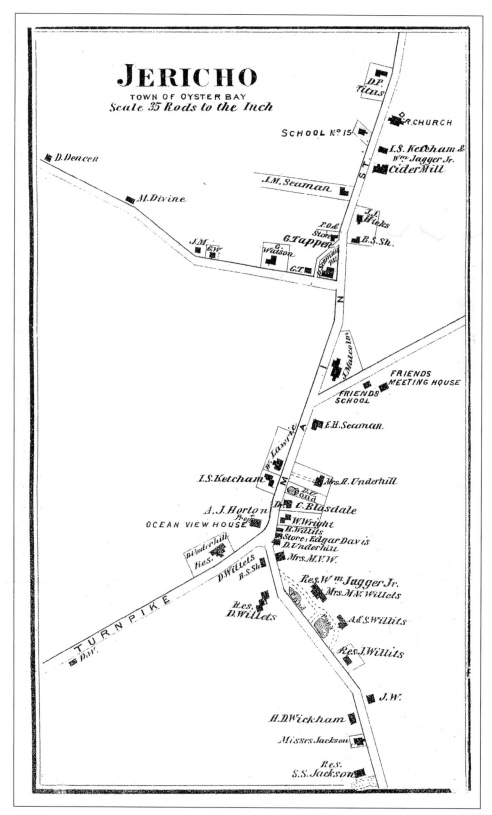

Jericho c 1873 (Beers, Comstock & Cline's Atlas of Long Island, New York; JPL Archives).

3 1489 00604 8928

JERICHO

THE HISTORY OF A
LONG ISLAND HAMLET

Betsey Murphy
Local History Librarian
Jericho Public Library

*Cover: Solomon Seaman Jackson and family, seated on their front
porch for formal portrait, c 1875 (J.H. Beal photograph, NYC; JPL Archives).*

© 2009 Jericho Public Library
1 Merry Lane, Jericho, NY 11753
First Edition Spring 2009 • All rights reserved
Design by Inger Gibb • Editing & Production by Rosalie Ink Publications
Printed in USA
Library of Congress Catalog Number: 2009923117
ISBN: 978-0-9799844-0-2 09799844-0-8

ACKNOWLEDGEMENTS

Many thanks to all those who have been helpful in the creation of this book, beginning with Mary Donor, the former Director of the Jericho Public Library. She supported my work and believed in its value to the public. The Library Board, our former Director John Bosco and current Director Barbara Kessler have also been very supportive. The Adult Reference Librarians who were bombarded with my requests for help with editing, proof-reading and general suggestions were all fabulous. The Children's Librarians gave me a lot of help with content and readability to make this book appealing to all age groups. I would have been totally lost without Carlos Munozospina and the other sympathetic members of the staff who helped me with computer and graphic support! And, my thanks to Betty Schwartz, who prepared the index.

Special thanks go to Kathryn Abbe, the former Clerk of the Quaker Meeting in Jericho, a skilled professional photographer and author. She has opened my eyes to a world I did not know existed. Also special thanks to Suzanne Valenza, an English teacher at the Jericho High School, who inspired my annual lecture and walking tour as well as the research for her students' "Our Town" assignment, and who was kind enough to do my grammar and punctu-ation editing on her own time.

For help with research questions, art and permissions, I am indebted to Howard Kroplick, Melba Halleran Neville, Sally Ganger and Betty Brown for their grandmother's priceless book, Thomas Kuehhas and Joseph Butler of the Oyster Bay Historical Society, Marge Blais at the Jericho Fire Department, the staff at the Jericho Post Office, David Sullivan of the Company of Military Historians, and Laura Kotsis at the Detroit Public Library.

Thanks as well to my obliging reviewers Denward Collins Jr., Natalie A. Naylor, Edward J. Smits and John A. Strong.

Heartfelt thanks to my wonderful editor Terry Walton for her encouragement, support and guidance along my path to publication, and to Inger Gibb, the talented graphic designer who pulled the artwork and text together into one beautiful book.

To all those who just listened to me, colleagues, family and friends, who gave me sup-port, advice, and kept me on track, I appreciated every word.

– Betsey Murphy

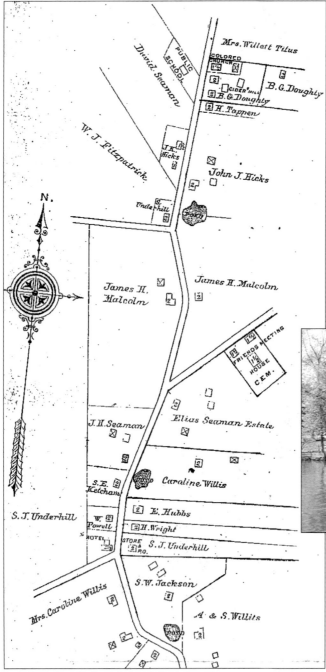

To the "Where is Jericho?" question I answer that the Milleridge Inn, a well-known landmark, is in Jericho. That answer usually brings an "Oh yes, now I know!"

Map of Jericho, 1906, showing Titus, Hicks, Seaman, Underhill, and Jackson properties and the Spring Pond. . . . Milleridge Inn and the Spring Pond with full complement of ducks, 1950s (map E. Belcher Hyde Atlas; photograph Milleridge Collection, JPL Archives).

To Kathryn Abbe—a dear friend
who introduced me to Old Jericho—
and to all the residents of Jericho past, present and future.

TIMELINE OF JERICHO HISTORY

40,000 years ago Pleistocene Ice Age

1644 Hempstead Compact is signed.

1648 The Robert Williams purchase. Williams acquires nine square miles of land—today's Jericho, Hicksville, Woodbury, and parts of Syosset —from the Matinecock Indians.

1660s The Williams family settles here in "Lusum" along with members of the Willets, Seaman and Jackson families. Most families built near the "Spring Pond," a natural source of drinking water. Robert Williams' widowed sister-in-law Mary Washburne Willets built the house by the Spring Pond that evolved into the Milleridge Inn.

1692 The area is named "Jericho."

1771 Elias Hicks and Jemima Seaman marry at the Westbury Friends Meeting House.

1788 Jericho Society of Friends Meeting House is built.

1793 Jericho Society of Friends School is built next to the Meeting House.

1794 The Charity Society of the Jericho and Westbury Monthly Meetings is formed.

1802 A Post Office is established in Jericho in the home of William Guthe.

1817 Slavery ends in Jericho.

1870 First Jericho public school is built on Oyster Bay Road (Route 106).

1890s Ketcham & Jagger Cider Mill is purchased by the Doughty family. In 1938 it was purchased by the Zulkofske family, who own and operate it today.

1915 Halleran brothers operate garage & blacksmith shop at the corner of Jericho Turnpike and the Hicksville– Oyster Bay Road.

1928-29 Jericho Turnpike is straightened.

1933 Volunteer Fire Department is established.

1936-38 Northern State Parkway is built through the southern part of the hamlet of Jericho.

1950s Center of Jericho bulldozed to widen Hicksville–Oyster Bay Road.

1952-62 Phebe Underhill Seaman, a great-great granddaughter of Elias Hicks, sells a large tract of land to developers. "Old Jericho" is demolished. The Spring Pond is filled in and Route 106/107 is widened. A traffic cloverleaf is constructed to provide access to and from Jericho Turnpike and Routes 106/107. More than 1,000 new houses are built in the area. The population of Jericho jumps from 600 to 12,000.

1958 New shopping center and new Post Office are built. New Fire Department building is dedicated on the 25th anniversary of the Jericho Fire Department.

1959 New high school complex on Cedar Swamp Road; opens February 1960.

1959 Long Island Expressway is extended though Jericho.

1966 Jericho Public Library opens.

1972 Jericho Preserve is created.

1972 Jericho Public Library's new building opens.

2006 Library celebrates 40th Anniversary.

2006-07 Underhill property is subdivided.

2007 New Firehouse is built on Broadway.

CONTENTS

ILLUSTRATIONS

INTRODUCTION

Where is Jericho? It's hard to explain the location of a community that was almost erased from the map in the 1950s—when the New York State Department of Transportation decided to widen the local road from Hicksville to Oyster Bay and bulldozed all the buildings in the center of the hamlet named Jericho. To the "Where is Jericho?" question I answer that the Milleridge Inn, a well-known landmark, is in Jericho. That answer usually brings an "Oh yes, now I know!"

Actually, Jericho is a small hamlet, just four square miles, situated in the middle of Nassau County about thirty miles east of midtown Manhattan. Its major attraction at the moment is its school system, which is ranked annually in *Newsweek* magazine as one of the best in America. Jericho High School can boast about its AP classes and Intel and other national science award competition winners, as well as its highly regarded computer, theater, music, dance, art and sports programs.

Many of Jericho's residents are "newcomers," as new generations have replaced the original Quaker settlers. There are nevertheless a few people here who can remember the "good old days" in Jericho before the bulldozers a half-century ago, and before the new houses in the new developments. Less than five years ago a new battle was waged, but only partially won, to preserve the wide open spaces of the Underhill property on Jericho Turnpike. Today, million dollar homes are being built side by side on half of the original property. The remaining half of the land is being preserved as permanent open space.

Thanks to our recent upsurge in new families, all too few of Jericho's current residents are even aware of our rich early history; of how hundreds of Quakers fled persecution in 17th century England. The Quakers found persecution again when they tried to settle in Puritan New England, so they came here to Long Island to seek religious freedom, peace and prosperity. They survived the French and Indian Wars, as well as British occupation of Long Island during the American Revolution—when British and Hessian troops lived in their houses and camped in their fields and on the Meeting House grounds.

The Jericho and neighboring Quakers like their counterparts in England were great advocates of freedom and education for all, male or female, black or white. They built schools, meeting houses and several businesses, and profoundly affected the towns in which they lived and prospered.

Jericho itself was an undisturbed and bucolic farmland when Jericho Turnpike was "straightened" in 1929. Then it was sliced through its southern portion by the Northern State Parkway in 1936-38, and in 1959 by the Long Island Expressway. The final blow came in the late 1950s when the old New York State Department of Transportation did its bull-dozing on the Hicksville–Oyster Bay Road. The new housing developments that mushroomed afterwards completed the transformation of the former rural hamlet to a busy suburbia. Jericho lacks a "center of town," yet honors the existing historic buildings in its Historic Preserve.

Only a handful of Jericho's residents now know there is an active 18th century Quaker Meeting House tucked away on Old Jericho Turnpike, or that the Jericho Historic Preserve—a twenty-acre site just north of Jericho Turnpike (Route 25) and east of Route 106—even exists. Few realize that the Jericho Cider Mill has been famous for its cider for over one hundred years, or that the famed Vanderbilt Cup Auto Races ran right through Jericho each fall from 1904 to 1908.

This history of Jericho has a twofold purpose. Its primary intention is to serve as a community information source for all who seek knowledge of Jericho's rich background, and for the numerous students who are assigned research on their home town of Jericho, and need a concise reference tool. This book confirms the original identity of a community that must never be lost in the changes and bustle of modern development.

My second intention has been to provide a personal history lesson for myself! When I became the Local History Librarian for the Jericho Public Library in 1991, the archives were already in place but had no "finding aids" to tell me what they held. Working part-time each week I spent several years just inventorying the amazingly rich contents of the collection. That work gave me an ongoing history lesson on Jericho and the rest of Long Island as well. I still learn something new every day from people who ask questions that I can't answer without further research, and I'm always relieved to find there is still an interest in the "Old Jericho."

I am particularly thrilled at the questions asked by students at my annual local history lecture. The curious ones are the impetus for the fervent research that went into this book! The text of this little history comes from many different papers I compiled on subjects that I researched to answer inquiries on local topics about which—as Local History Librarian— I needed to know. It will never be a complete history, and probably will have to be revised in the future, because intriguing new facts continually come to light. But for now I hope it will serve the purposes for which it is intended.

– Betsey Murphy
Jericho Public Library, 2009

Watercolor of Malcolm Barns by Alphonso Gallo, 1968 (JPL purchase, 1975).

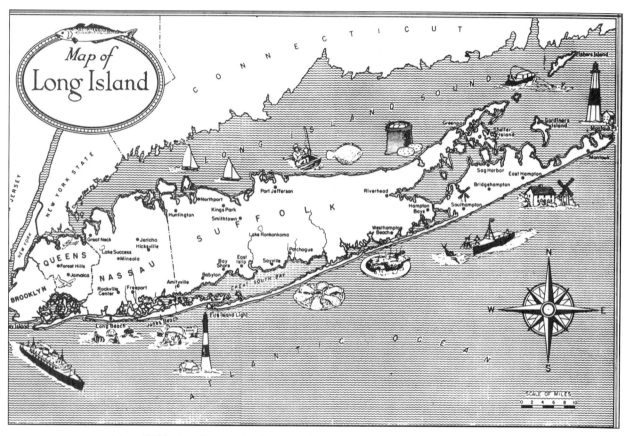

Map of "fish-shape" Long Island (Mannello's Our Long Island, *reprinted with permission).*

---

*The North Shore of Long Island
is a tall bluff, indented by bays and inlets
offering safe harbors as well as necks or
peninsulas jutting out into the Sound.*

GEOGRAPHY & GEOLOGY OF LONG ISLAND 1

I do remember alternating periods of hot and cold years, and wet and dry ones. I think that occurs all over the world. Perhaps there has been a slight ameliorating of the climate. The plants and the invasion of birds show more than your own senses do because it's a very gradual and slow change.
—Oral history transcript of Barbara Hewlett Connolly, Jericho resident, 1975

Well, I think it's generally known that during the early glacial period the glaciers moving out of New England, coming down gouged out Long Island and pushed it up. Most of Long Island is a sandbar anyway and these glaciers stopped right about the Jericho Line.
—Oral history transcript of George Doughty, resident and owner of Jericho Cider Mill, 1975

Geologists say that Long Island, with its fish-like shape, was formed from glacial debris carried from Connecticut and Westchester by a moving glacier, during the last stage of the Pleistocene Ice Age about 40,000 years ago. The island may have remained under water until it was finally pushed upward in the Wisconsin Glacial Stage, named for an archeological study done in that state on rocks similar to the ones found on Long Island. Today's Jericho retains clear legacies from this ancient time.

As is well known, the Wisconsin Glacier covered most of North America, including Long Island, in two separate layers. The first time the glacier pushed its way toward the Atlantic Ocean it deposited huge amounts of debris in the form of large boulders, rocks, gravel, soil and sand. (One of these boulders would be carved in prehistoric times and later known as the Jericho Petroglyph.) Then the earth's temperature warmed, and the ice slowly receded at the rate of one or two miles per century. On Long Island, water from melting ice ran toward the ocean—creating the flat plains of the South Shore, in the southern part of today's Jericho, a treeless prairie called the Hempstead Plains.

Temperatures dropped again over the years and the Wisconsin Glacier reformed, once again moving south across Long Island. This time the ice didn't reach the ocean on the South Shore, but it carved out "kettle holes," both large and small, that later evolved into lakes and ponds. When the ice receded again some small kettle holes simply dried up—but there are still a few small kettle hole ponds left in Jericho. The largest ones remaining on Long Island are familiar to us all—Lake Ronkonkoma and Lake Success.

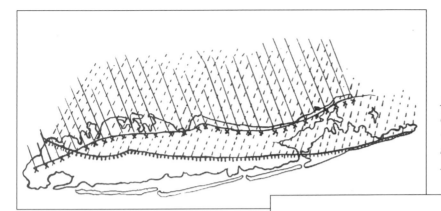

Map of Long Island showing it covered by ice during Wisconsin stage of the Glacier period. Heavy horizontal lines trace paths of Ronkonkoma and Harbor Hill moraines (Voelbel, 1963).

Diagram of a kettle hole formation. Large chunks of ice broke off from the glacier and became buried under sand and gravel. Eventually the ice melted. Some holes became dry ravines, but others fed by underground springs became lakes and ponds, such as Lake Ronkonkoma and Lake Success (graphic, B. Murphy).

A - Formation of a Kettle Hole from an ice mass.
B - Kettle Hole pond left after ice mass melted.

The receding glacier also left behind lengthy stretches of debris that formed a long ridge of small hills, some as high as three-hundred-fifty feet, called the Long Island terminal moraines and stretching like a fish's backbone the full length of the island. Historian Paul Bailey reports in his book *Physical Long Island* that the Harbor Hill Moraine crosses the northern part of Jericho and ends out east on the North Fork of the Island, and the Ronkonkoma Moraine ends on the South Fork.

The North Shore of Long Island is a tall bluff, indented by bays and inlets offering safe harbors as well as necks or peninsulas jutting out into the Sound. The same melting glacier caused the sea level to rise against this bluff, flooding the lowlands to create the Long Island Sound—a permanent water separation between Long Island and Connecticut. Today it is a popular recreation site and a water route to New York City, Westchester and New England.

Peter Ross describes Long Island's geology in his book *The History of Long Island* as being a mixture of gravel, coarse sand, a variety of clays ranging from fine white to heavy red and brown, and an amazing number of different kinds of rock—some of which date back billions of years. Garnet, sandstone, quartz, slate, mica, feldspar, granite and limestone deposits have been found here. Magnetite, the only metallic ore found on Long Island, is in the sand on our beaches but is not abundant enough to be collected for profit. Several large deposits of fine white pottery clay and heavy brick-making clay were the sources for profitable pottery and brick industries in both Nassau and Suffolk counties in the late 1800s and early 1900s. Glen Cove had a large deposit of fine pottery clay. Manetto Hill had a brickworks, and Huntington's Cold Spring Harbor was the site of the Crossman and the Jones brickyards—which produced nearly twenty million bricks until they ran out of firewood to burn in their kilns.

The glacier also left behind fertile soil leading to a great assortment of vegetation and wildlife, which has varied over the centuries in response to human intervention. Long Island has always been known for its farms, and is now known for its vineyards too. Multiple sources of pure water from natural springs added to the land's fertility. The Island's many rivers and streams flowing into its bays would soon provide food and shelter for beavers, ducks, geese and other waterfowl, and serve as an excellent breeding ground for shellfish.

The South Shore's barrier beaches helped create vast tracts of salt marshes and meadows, giving shelter to waterfowl and the nourishing grasses that were fodder for domesticated farm animals. Wild deer, turkeys, foxes, muskrats and squirrels were abundant. Large stands of white cedar, hemlocks, maples and chestnut trees flourished. Oak, hickory, spruce and tulip trees soon followed. Out east, nearly 100,000 protected acres of what are today called the Pine Barrens are habitat for birds and small animals.

The Island's many rivers and streams flowing into its bays would soon provide food and shelter for beavers, ducks, geese and other waterfowl, and serve as an excellent breeding ground for shellfish.

At mid-island, the sixteen-mile-long prairie-like Hempstead Plains, where trees didn't seem to grow, had its own varieties of flora and fauna. Paul Bailey writes further that some believe the Algonquian Indians, our predecessors here, may have repeatedly burned clear parts of the grassy Plains to plant crops. Early European settlers had a limited supply of tools and laborers, which limited the size of their planting fields. Quotes from Daniel Denton's 1670 *A Brief Description of New York* describe the Plain "upon which grows very fine grass that makes exceeding good hay, and is very good pasture for sheep or other cattle." The colonists found it perfect for horse racing, a favorite pastime, as well as for pastureland, because it was so flat and lacked the multitude of glacial-deposit stones found closer to the North Shore.

Long Island's year-round temperate climate, aided by the surrounding waters of ocean and Sound, added further appeal to animal and human habitation. □

A HAPPY FAMILY.

Native Americans hunted the abundant wildlife on Long Island— deer, beaver, squirrels, and even bear (Harpers Monthly Magazine, *1858, JPL Archives*).

INDIAN WOMEN MAKING WAMPUM

Wampum, here being hand cut from shells by Native American women, was used for ornaments and currency (JPL Archives).

The Jericho Petroglyph—a granite boulder with ancient carvings of star, triangle and bow and arrow. It was found in 1975 just north of the LIE in Jericho, split in two most likely by weather. Similar petroglyphs have been authenticated in New Jersey, Pennsylvania and the upper Ohio River valley (JPL Archives).

Long Island's Native Americans 2

All the ethnographic data on the North American cultures . . . suggest that they identified themselves in terms of lineage and clan membership. These village communities did not have clearly defined, hierarchical political structures, with rulers who could command absolute obedience from their followers. The borders of their hunting territories were very loosely drawn.
—*The Algonquian Peoples of Long Island,* John A. Strong, 1997

Q: *Did you ever find any Indian artifacts near the house?*
A: *Well, down in the field we found two or three arrowheads, but that was all.*
—Oral History Transcript of Phebe Underhill Smith, Jericho resident, 1974

The first human beings appeared in Jericho and all of Long Island between six and ten thousand years ago during the Paleo Period, and thus are named Paleo-Indians by anthropologists, but they had no written language, so they left no history from their perspective.

Historians such as Paul Bailey, George Mannello, Jacqueline Overton and Peter Ross mistakenly referred to the thirteen Indian "tribes" on Long Island. John Morice used the term "geographic place-names" such as the "Peconics" or "Canarsies" rather than tribal names. Later studies made by John Strong and others have made it quite clear there were no tribal systems on Long Island prior to the 1650s, when native groups banded together for survival purposes after contact with the European colonists. The Indians, being nomadic, separated into groups in certain localities, but usually did not remain too long in the same spot.

Mannello states that the Native Americans of Long Island welcomed the arriving Europeans in the early 1600s, and enjoyed trading with them. They greeted the white men as equals, and were treated by the white men with the same courtesy, in the beginning. Both sides were pleased with the trading of pelts and food for blankets and trinkets. The rich fur pelts of fox, beaver and otter that the Indians traded to the Europeans encouraged more and more traders and trappers to the New World.

European settlers came to the New World for another reason as well: the prospect of owning property, which only the wealthy could do in their homeland. The Indians were happy to "sell" their land to the white settlers because they didn't recognize the European concept of selling or owning land. Their religion taught them that the land belongs to Manitou, the Supreme Being, and no one person could own it. The land was here for the benefit of all to share and enjoy while they were living on it. These beliefs led to frequent disputes between natives and newcomers.

Over the centuries the Native Americans became skilled hunters, shell fishermen and even whalers. They later became planters and growers of tobacco, corn, beans, squash and useful herbs. They studied the moon and the stars, developed religious rites and carved sacred idols and tablets, both large and small. The Jericho Petroglyph, just north of the Long Island Expressway, has five images carved on one side—a hand, a star, a bow and arrow, and a triangular hole that may have been retouched later—and was verified in 1975 as dating back to the Indians of the Late Woodland Period.

Anthropologists report that the Native Americans on Long Island had a well-developed culture and led industrious lives. They played complex games, told stories and enjoyed informal singing. To keep peace, they paid tribute to the more aggressive Indians on the mainland of New York and Connecticut to prevent raiding parties from kidnapping their family members and holding them for ransom.

The highly prized beads called wampum served as money for ransoms, and as payment to settle debts and grievances. Wampum was also used as gifts, to negotiate treaties, to honor people in ceremonies and to buy brides from other tribes. It was easy to carry and was accepted as currency by the Dutch and the English as well.

Over the centuries the Native Americans became skilled hunters, shell fishermen and even whalers.

Wampum beads were cut by hand from the hard seashells of the conch, quahog clam and whelk and often strung together and used for adornment by men and women as belts and necklaces. This display of wampum distinguished the wealthy and proud from the poor and humble. It was the basis of the Native American economy as well as a symbol of honor and respect. Its value would later decrease when it was mass produced.

The disastrous impact of disease, the conflict of cultures and understandings about "sold" land, and the murderous Dutch raids on the Indians under Governor Kieft from 1640 to 1645 drastically reduced Long Island's Native American population. These kinds of problems, as well as the taxes forced on the Indians by the Dutch, increased the difficulties between natives and colonists. John Strong documents that after years of bloody Dutch and Indian conflicts from Rhode Island to New Jersey, Dutch Governor Kieft's actions toward the Indians led them to retaliate—nearly destroying the Dutch settlements on Long Island and leading to Indians being widely massacred. Records confirm that a treaty was signed in 1645 but tension and violence continued for many years.

So, diverse political, cultural and medical factors contributed to decimation of the Native American population. The Indians paid a heavy price for their contact with the Europeans. □

THE DUTCH SETTLERS
ON LONG ISLAND 3

Hitherto the Dutch had looked on Manhattan only as a trading-post.
They did not think of making themselves homes in this new, wild country. . . .
But the English were exploring the coast and laying claim to all the country
between Canada and Virginia, and the Dutch began to realize the importance of planting
colonies in the new province, and thus securing their American possessions.
—*History of the City of New York*, Mary L. Booth, 1859

Every school child has learned about the European search for a route to the Far East that led to the "discovery" of America. Columbus was sent by Spain in 1492 and John Cabot by the English in 1497. Cabot, and later his son Sebastian in 1508, claimed all the land on the Atlantic coast for England. In 1524, France sent Giovanni da Verazzano to our shores to find a Northwest Passage.

Nearly one hundred years later, in 1609, the Dutch East India Company sent an Englishman, Henry Hudson, who claimed all the territory he saw—what is now New York, New Jersey, Delaware and part of Connecticut—for the Dutch, who named it "New Netherland." About five years later, Adriaen Block established a Dutch fur trading outpost in the New World. Block explored Long Island, named a small island for himself and drew a map of "Lange Eylandt" showing that it actually was an island. By 1624 the Dutch had erected a small fort on Manhattan to protect the settlement with its four small houses. The Dutch traded beads, cotton cloth and other goods for the natives' beaver, otter and mink pelts.

The English meanwhile had created a permanent settlement in Jamestown, Virginia, in 1607 and in 1620 the Plymouth Colony in Massachusetts, establishing a substantial English presence in the New World. But the newly formed Dutch West India Company pressed on and by 1626 had sent a group of approximately two hundred Dutch, to settle on the island of Manhattan, which was then named "New Amsterdam."

The colonists were eager to learn from and peacefully coexist with the native population. Some even learned the local language and farming methods and—as noted—used the wampum system for money. The colonial economy relied so heavily on the furs the Indians trapped that the entire Northeastern beaver population neared extinction over the years.

According to historian Peter Ross, the Dutch West India Company was so eager to have

VIEW IN NEW YORK, 1769

Typical Dutch architectural styles brought to New Netherland (History of City of New York, *1859;* A Tour Around New York, *1893, JPL Archives).*

PETERSFIELD, THE RESIDENCE OF PETRUS STUYVESANT

Sketch of Peter Stuyvesant's house (A Tour Around New York, *1893, JPL Archives).*

their colony succeed that they promised to provide as "many blacks as they conveniently can" to assist in construction and to work on the Dutch farms. So African slavery was introduced to this region as early as 1626.

It was in 1636, historians report, that the first Dutch settlers extended their holdings across the East River onto Long Island. But controversy continued to grow between the Dutch and the English over rights to this growing colony. The Dutch held the reins of government, but England based its property claims on Cabot's earlier discovery of the east coast region, and on a land grant issued by King James I covering that territory. Both countries encouraged more immigration, and more permanent settlements to strengthen the authority of their claims.

At the same time, groups of outcast Puritans and discontented English settlers from Connecticut and Massachusetts tried to settle on Long Island. The quickest and easiest form of travel in those days was by water, and the trip across Long Island Sound by boat was not too difficult a journey. The Dutch expelled several groups of "unauthorized" English settlers but some managed to settle further out on eastern Long Island.

In 1643-44, approximately forty English families purchased land from the Indians, obtained a land patent from the Dutch and founded the town of Hempstead—which encompassed all of today's towns of Hempstead, North Hempstead and the Rockaway Peninsula (now part of Queens). Among these English settlers were families named Denton, Underhill, Jackson, Seaman and, later, Williams, Washburne, Willets and Hicks, who would establish a legacy that lives on in our area today.

In all of New Netherland, however, the English were subject to Dutch rule, as were the Swedes, Germans and an amazing variety of other nationalities who had settled there. As can be seen in the mixture of ethnic backgrounds in the court and marriage records of New Amsterdam, the colony itself had become a true "melting pot" of nationalities and races, who lived and worked together and intermarried. For the most part the colonists were able to live side by side. They accepted each other's religions, seeing the importance of preserving religion as an aspect of maintaining order in the community, but dealt severely with "dissidents," and so-called heretics.

In Hempstead the English settlers were allowed to elect their own magistrates, but continued to assert their rights against the oppression of the Dutch Governor Peter Stuyvesant and his Council. Religion was restricted to the Dutch Reformed and a few acceptable Protestant churches, including Presbyterian and Congregational. Taxes and tariffs seemed exorbitant and trade goods, by law, had to come from Holland.

For the most part the colonists were able to live side by side. They accepted each other's religions, seeing the importance of preserving religion as an aspect of maintaining order in the community.

The Dutch West India Company finally ordered Stuyvesant to negotiate a settlement of various land disputes with the English. In 1650, the Treaty of Hartford mandated that the English would own the land east of Oyster Bay on Long Island, and the Connecticut River Valley east of Greenwich. The western part of New Netherland would remain Dutch.

But despite the treaty England persisted in her claim to the whole territory. Ten years afterwards, in 1660, King Charles II gave James, the Duke of York, a written land grant for all territory between the Connecticut River and the Delaware River. James sent an impressive fleet, under command of Colonel Richard Nicolls, to take control of the colony. Governor Stuyvesant reluctantly surrendered the colony in August 1664. Many Dutch settlers chose to remain on their property under the new English regime and their presence is seen today in the Dutch colonial architecture and Dutch names like Onderdonk, Hegeman and Schenck that are so familiar to us on Long Island. □

Copy of 1648 Williams Plantation purchase agreement (JPL Archives).

THE ROBERT WILLIAMS STORY

4

*The next evidence of a settlement by Europeans in the territory now the Town
of Oysterbay appears in a deed by a certain of the Aborigines to Robert Williams dated
May 20th, 1648, including and conveying a certain tract bounded generally north
by the Ridge of Hills about Jericho, east by the woods and west by the Point of Trees called
Cantiage; for which a patent was issued by Governor Richard Nicolls in 1666.*

—Oyster Bay Town Records, 1653-1690

Little is known about Robert Williams, the credited founder of Jericho,
so his story here has been gathered from the available research. We know
he was a son of a man named Thomas Williams, and is reported to have emigrated from Lewisham, England, to an unspecified part of the New England
area around 1630—roughly a decade after the Pilgrims landed.

Mary Thomas Seaman, a descendant of Robert Williams, writes that
there is no documented proof either way, that Williams was of Welsh
descent, the brother of Richard Williams of Huntington, Long Island, or
else a relative of Roger Williams of Rhode Island, as is reported in several local histories.
Records clearly show that he was married to Sarah Washburne, the daughter of William and
Jane Washburne, and—a few years after the Hempstead Compact—was allocated six acres
of property in Hempstead—the usual procedure for new settlers in those days.

By 1647, when he was a successful middle-aged businessman and the father of seven or
eight children, Hempstead Town Records list Robert Williams as a cattle owner and carpenter, a trade he probably learned in England. He was ambitious, a man of vision, close to the
equivalent of today's real estate developer. In later years we find records of his land acquisi-
tions near today's Glen Cove, Massapequa, Oyster Bay and Huntington, making him one
of Long Island's most prominent landowners of the day.

One indication of his wealth and personal influence was his ability to "purchase" a very
large parcel of land from the Algonquians in 1648 in the eastern part of the area
called The Hempstead Plains. The agreement was signed by the local sachem Pugnipan,
with eight other Native Americans, and Robert Williams, with two of his English friends,
under the grand oak tree at Cantiag (Cantiague) Woods. The Williams purchase was
roughly nine square miles, or six thousand acres, casually measured by landmarks—a tree
here, a stream there—rather than by any more formal methods. In exchange for a quantity
of cloth and some appealing trinkets, Williams acquired the areas that are now called

Cantiague Rock marks the site where Robert Williams signed an agreement with the sachem Pugnipan to purchase the Williams Plantation, May 20, 1648 (Braner Collection, JPL Archives). . . . Re-enactment (1976) of the 1648 Williams Plantation purchase (Braner Collection, JPL Archives).

By 1658, Williams was documented as the third largest taxpayer in Hempstead—unequivocal evidence of his prosperity.

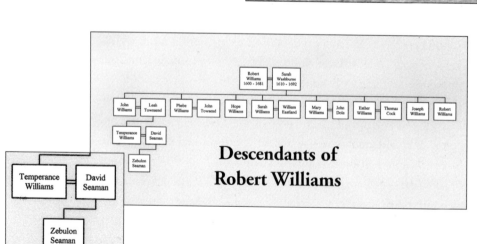

Descendants of Robert Williams

In Williams family tree, descendants of Robert Williams appear at lower left—ending with Temperance Williams marrying David Seaman, patriarch of many Jericho families (JPL Archives).

Jericho, Hicksville, Plainview, Woodbury and part of Syosset. This area would for a time be known as "The Plantation," part of the Town of Oyster Bay.

The original deed, dated May 20, 1648, was not found in the Dutch records in New Amsterdam, probably because the Dutch were still in control of this area, and Williams wanted to keep this purchase quiet because the English settlers were still living under Dutch rule. When the English took control of the colony twenty years later, an official, or "true," copy would be recorded in the British Office of Records in New York on February 12, 1666.

But Robert Williams did not stop with the six-thousand-acre 1648 purchase. Just five years later in 1653, Richard Houlbrock, Daniel Whitehead and Robert Williams made a deal with the Matinecock Indian sachem Asharoken for a large tract of land between Cold Spring and Northport harbors—about six square miles—for the area that would later become Huntington. Williams didn't keep his shares, but sold them to other settlers soon afterward—undoubtedly a good investment.

Robert Williams's name was also found on other land purchase records in Oyster Bay in 1653 when a boat filled with pioneers from Rhode Island landed in Oyster Bay. The names of these newcomers, Peter Wright—"Founder" of Oyster Bay—Reverend William Leverich and Samuel Mayo were listed on a new land acquisition from the Algonquian Indians, along with Robert Williams as "a joynt purchaser." We can assume that these men knew Williams earlier in New England (Oyster Bay records note that Wright became a lifelong friend) and came to Long Island by prearranged plan.

By 1658, Williams was documented as the third largest taxpayer in Hempstead—unequivocal evidence of his prosperity. The Williams family moved to Oyster Bay about 1660, to secure his holdings there. Five years later he sold his home and cattle in Hempstead to Henry Pearsall, and was admitted as a freeholder in the Town of Oyster Bay. Within a year, he obtained a proper English land patent from Governor Andros confirming his ownership of the Hempstead Plains Plantation—known as Lusum and later called Jericho—enabling him to "sell to and plant so many families as need."

The Williams Plantation had a source of pure spring water, fertile land for crops, abundant fields of grass for cattle—and plenty of wood for building houses and barns.

In 1667, according to Oyster Bay Records, Williams now purchased a third piece of land from a John Richbell in Oyster Bay. Still another record lists "Robert Williams of Oyster Bay" giving some of his property in Jericho to his recently widowed sister-in-law Mary Washburne Willets. That same year he moved his wife Sarah and two of his sons, John and Hope, to the Plantation, along with his sister-in-law Mary and two of her sons. The deed refers to a house located on "ye east side of ye highway and against ye hill." In modern terms this translates to the east side of Broadway, slightly north of the very vital Spring Pond by the Mary Washburn Willets house.

The Williams Plantation had a source of pure spring water, fertile land for crops, abundant fields of grass for cattle—and plenty of wood for building houses and barns. Robert invited a few other families to settle there with them to develop his claim. He must have soon had

Underhill Ice House still stands on the Underhill property. A similar one may be seen on the Malcolm property in the Historic Preserve (1971 photograph, Underhill Collection, JPL Archives). . . . In winter, large blocks of ice cut from the Spring Pond were carted home for underground ice houses, the "refrigerators" of the day (Doughty print from glass plate negative c 1890, JPL Archives).

The Spring Pond, naturally fed by pure underground springs, attracted Robert Williams to settle in Jericho. People came from miles around to fill their carts with fresh drinking water (Korten postcard, c 1903, Harry Stewart Collection, JPL Archives).

several families living there; by 1668 he had enough influence with Governor Nicolls to get one male member of each of the households on his Plantation exempted from militia service. It's unlikely that Williams cultivated much of his property, perhaps due to a limited supply of tools and available labor and the fact that he was not by trade a farmer. The land was used mainly for grazing large herds of cattle, probably sheep, goats and the necessary chickens and geese. Vegetable gardens and fruit trees were planted to feed the families. Flax was spun for clothing and linens.

In 1684, as noted in the Oyster Bay Town Records, Jericho was "a place to enter the woods from the plains" called "Lewsum," or "Lusum." This may have been a derivative of "Lewisham," the area in Great Britain where the Williams family once lived. Some sources claim that "Lussum" is a Native American word meaning "farms." The area is also called "The Farms," or "Lusam" or even "Springfield" at different times and in different records of the day.

The well-established Robert Williams spent his remaining years buying and selling property in the Oyster Bay area, though official records show that he did not divide or dispose of much land within the Plantation. The Town of Oyster Bay Records mention an attempt to change the casual boundary markers of trees and rocks to more precise boundaries between the Oyster Bay Purchase and the Williams Plantation adjacent to it. It was in 1692 that an area within the Plantation was named Jericho, making it one of the four "Bible" towns of Long Island—along with Bethpage, Babylon and Jerusalem, now called Wantagh.

Williams had died a decade earlier in around 1681 during a trip to Kent County, Maryland, but no record of his burial place has yet been located. His wife Sarah Washburne Williams continued to live in their home by the Spring Pond in Jericho until her death in about 1692. Regrettably, the house does not survive today; Robert Seaman's account tells us that it was torn down in 1928.

John, one of the Williams's sons, married Leah Townsend. Their daughter Hannah grew up to marry John Seaman and they became the grandparents of Jemima Seaman, wife of the famous Quaker Elias Hicks.

There is quite a bit of evidence that Robert Williams was a Quaker, though probably not a formally professed one. This gives some credence to the aforementioned idea that he was related to Roger Williams of Rhode Island, who was famous for his liberal religious beliefs. It is known that most of Robert Williams's friends and associates were Quakers, and many of them had been persecuted for their religious beliefs.

According to Bailey's *History of Long Island*, the Plantation was handed down to Robert Williams's children and grandchildren. The land was formally divided in 1746, using a survey prepared by Samuel Willis. Not one single family with the surname of Williams was among the sixty landowners living there at that time, which contributes still more mystery to Robert Williams's life story. □

Solomon Seaman Jackson and family, c 1875, on front porch of their home, which stood just east of the Jericho-Hicksville Road (Broadway today) near where the LIE now cuts through Jericho (J. H. Beal, photographer NYC, JPL Archives).

Above left: Solomon Seaman Jackson (1817-1905), head of an early Quaker family in Jericho (JPL Archives, from original at Friends Academy). . . . Solomon Seaman Jackson family portrait with his second wife Esther Post and their daughter Caroline Underhill Jackson, and his other children, Ancel, Solomon, Francis P. and Grace Anna by his first wife Annie (J. H. Beal, photographer NYC, c 1880, JPL Archives).

EARLY QUAKER SETTLERS IN JERICHO 5

Jericho is situated six miles south of Oysterbay, near the north-east corner of the Great Plain, on the Jericho Turnpike. It was settled at an early period, principally by Friends, and that is the only denomination that has a house of worship there.
—*A History of Long Island*, Nathaniel S. Prime, 1845

Most Quakers, or Members of the Religious Society of Friends, were moderately prosperous people who regularly repudiated privilege and aristocracy. They strongly believed that honesty and plain-dealing were fundamental to life itself. Business failure or indebtedness was proof one had strayed away from Quaker ways.

In the mid-17th century the English government barred Quakers from many professions and from educational institutions, because they were religious dissenters—so the Friends turned to business and opened their own schools. James Surowiecki in *The Wisdom of Crowds* writes that Quakers in the late 1700s and early 1800s controlled a significant portion of Great Britain's economy. They were influential in banking, overseas trade and shipping, and in consumer businesses like chocolate, biscuits, iron and coal. Today's famed Cadbury Chocolates were among their business successes.

Because of the Quakers' excellent reputation for honesty, their practice of fixed prices over special deals and their scrupulous bookkeeping, even non-Quakers sought to do business with them. As their prosperity rose their reputation for fair deals and honesty rose as well.

When they decided to seek religious freedom in America, Quakers differed from many of the impoverished or indentured immigrants; they could acquire property and establish businesses despite the extreme persecution and prejudice they had endured—both here and in England in the early days. As a general practice, most Quakers kept in regular contact with each other. They formed networks between local Meetings, wrote to each other frequently and exchanged publications. Hospitality and welcome were assured to all Friends in both their commercial and their social travels.

Another aspect of their religious practice was the rule that a Quaker could marry only another member of the Quaker faith. Researchers often find a confusing interconnection of family names and family names used as first names—and thus a challenge in confirming exactly who is descended from whom!

There were many Quaker family names in early Jericho and surrounding towns; only a

"The Houses are Large and Comfortable, in a Plain Way . . ."

Jericho . . . has always been the home of a group of prosperous Quaker families, most of whom inherited their substance. . . . The houses are large and comfortable, in a plain way, and as long back as I can remember there were flower gardens. . . . It was almost necessary to have vegetable gardens and fruit trees, for nothing of the kind was ever for sale. Several of the homes had large and fine farms in connection, on which agricultural work was done, but I suspect, with very little profit. The largest and finest estate was that of Daniel Underhill, and their home, too, was the largest and most elaborate. . . . The next best farm was that of Solomon Jackson, where the house was built on the first rise from the level plains to the south. . . . The Elias Seaman home was not a farm, nor was our place, but each was large enough for outbuildings, gardens and orchards. The Malcolm place topped the next rise to the north and was the oldest and most interesting home in Jericho. That place had only the necessary land for gardens, pastures for cows and horses, etc. The house must have been late 1700, for the ceilings were low and the rooms small, which was the case where heating facilities were very inadequate.

Next to our home on the north was the residence of Elias Hicks, now, in all Jericho, the one place nearest its original condition, and it is occupied by his great granddaughter, Anna Seaman. There were two other homes of importance, the old Jackson and Willits places, one behind and one beside the Big Pond.

—Family Affairs or Go to Jericho, Phebe Ketcham McAllister, 1939

few of the most notable ones are included in this chapter. These Quaker names are the source of many Long Island streets and places we know well today—among them Jackson Avenue, Titus Lane, Underhill Boulevard and Hicksville.

The Hicks Family

The original John Hicks emigrated from England about 1639, and eventually settled in the Flushing and Hempstead area—where he became a magistrate and judge. John's son Thomas received a land grant in 1666 for several thousand acres around Great Neck, and was the great-great grandfather of Edward Hicks, the noted painter. An obituary in the *New York Postboy* on January 26, 1749, reported that over many generations, Thomas "left behind him, of his own offspring, above three hundred." Thomas's son Jacob was born in 1669 and would later settle in Rockaway, where his great grandson Elias Hicks, the famous Quaker preacher of Jericho, was born.

Elias was the son of a declared Quaker, John Hicks, and his wife, Martha Smith, but he did not become a practicing Quaker until his late teens when his family left Rockaway for the more flourishing Quaker community of Westbury. He married Jemima Seaman at the Westbury Meeting House in 1771. They had eleven children, but their four sons all died before reaching maturity. Their daughter Martha married Royal Aldrich and lived nearby, on Jericho Turnpike, in a house Elias gave to them. Elias's daughter Phebe married Joshua Willets, and her sister Sarah married Robert Seaman. Another daughter, Abigail, married her second cousin, Valentine Hicks, son of Isaac Hicks and Phebe Seaman Hicks. Valentine

Valentine Hicks home c 1850 with family members on the lawn. The house became Mr. and Mrs. Percy Roberts' Maine Maid Inn in early 1950s (JPL Archives).

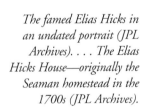

The famed Elias Hicks in an undated portrait (JPL Archives). . . . The Elias Hicks House—originally the Seaman homestead in the 1700s (JPL Archives).

Wedding photograph of Annie Titus Jackson and Matthew Franklin Jackson, October 10, 1894. Annie and M. Franklin were married at her parents' home in Jericho, and it is told they went to Niagara Falls on their honeymoon trip (JPL Archives).

The Marion Jackson house, built for her parents Annie and Matthew Franklin Jackson c 1895, stood on the Oyster Bay-Hicksville Road (today Broadway), near where the newest Firehouse is today. Marion lived here for her entire life with her mother Annie and her bachelor uncle George A. Jackson. At Marion's death the house was declared a landmark, and moved to the grounds of Friends Academy in 1989 (Kathryn Abbe photograph c 1950, JPL Archives).

and Abigail's son Elias became the president of the Chamber of Commerce of New York City.

More details about Elias Hicks, his family and his zealous work as a Quaker preacher in the time of slavery are found in a later chapter. His house still stands as a landmark on Old Jericho Turnpike. The Jericho Meeting House in which Elias Hicks preached—over 200 years old—is still in use today. It stands adjacent to the Jericho Historic Preserve.

The Jackson Family

Robert Jackson was another English immigrant who left Massachusetts to settle in Hempstead in the mid 1600s. He and his neighbor Captain John Seaman became two of the largest landholders in that town, and both men served in several official capacities. Robert Jackson married Agnes Washburne, another sister-in-law of Jericho founder Robert Williams, and their son John married Elizabeth Seaman, the daughter of John Seaman, their neighbor.

Many years and five generations later, Solomon Seaman Jackson married Annie Smithson Titus in Jericho. Their home stood on the east side of Broadway near the site of the newest Jericho Firehouse. The house was declared a landmark and in 1989 was moved to the campus of Friends Academy in Locust Valley. Their son Ancel Titus Jackson was the father of George A. Jackson, who worked as a banker in New York City. When George retired he became treasurer of the Jericho Public Schools. A public elementary school, on Maytime Drive, was named for him in 1957.

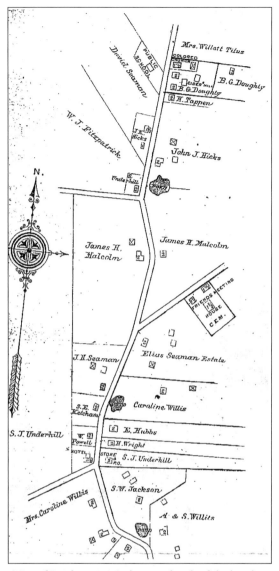

Map of Jericho c 1906, showing details of the hamlet at that time (JPL Archives).

The Seaman Family

In 1630, John Seaman left Essex, England, and sailed with Governor John Winthrop to the Massachusetts Bay Colony. He left Salem to relocate to Connecticut in 1636, where he is recorded as one of the original purchasers of Stamford in 1641. He became Captain of one of the Connecticut Troops in 1637 during the Pequot Indian Wars and married Elizabeth Strickland in 1644. They had five children. He was one of the sixty-two original signers (in Connecticut) of the Hempstead Compact in 1644 and settled there in 1647.

Captain John Seaman's family, after his second marriage to Martha Moore in 1655, grew to eight sons and eight daughters. In 1666 he settled the village of Jerusalem in Hempstead, on 2,200 acres of property that was practically a community in itself.

The family became members of the Society of Friends in about 1686. John Seaman Jr

The Robert Seaman house, c 1948, corner of Jericho Turnpike and Broadway across from the Milleridge Inn. The house was demolished in the 1950s for the cloverleaf (Tollaver Collection, JPL Archives). . . . Florence Bates (age 6) and Phebe Underhill Seaman (11 months) were raised together in the Robert Seaman home, while Florence's mother, Jennie, worked for the Seaman family (L. Hallock, photographer NYC, Tollaver Collection c 1897, JPL Archives).

married Hannah Williams, a daughter of Robert Williams. John and Hannah's son Benjamin Seaman married Martha Titus, and their daughter, Elizabeth, married their neighbor John Jackson.

Many generations later, Robert Seaman, a civic-minded man and the great grandson of Elias Hicks, served as Jericho's eleventh Postmaster from 1890 to 1894. He was one of the founding trustees of Jericho School District Number 15 in 1907, and financed the second public school building with local leaders James Malcolm and Emma A. Underhill. He attended the 1953 dedication of the Robert Seaman Public Grade School built on the site of his former property on Leahy Street, west of the Milleridge Inn.

Robert Seaman's daughter Phebe Underhill Seaman sold her land on the south side of Jericho Turnpike to a developer in 1952, which marked the beginning of the change in Jericho's landscape from rural to suburban.

The Titus Family

Robert and Hannah Carter Titus, along with their sons Edmond and John, sailed from London on the ship *Hopewell* in 1635 to the Massachusetts Bay Colony. Like so many others they sought to escape the religious strife so rampant in England. They moved from the Boston area to Weymouth and then to Rehoboth, part of the Plymouth Colony that was a haven of religious tolerance. In 1650, young Edmond left the Rehoboth church with a group of forty people and walked all the way to Long Island, where he settled in Hempstead and met his wife, Martha Washburne, a sister-in-law of Jericho's founder Robert Williams.

Edmond's Quaker parents, Robert and Hannah, would be "voted out" of Rehoboth in

1654, for harboring a family associated with Anne Hutchinson's ardent religious group. They settled in Huntington with their younger children, Abiel and Content, in a new English congregation.

Edmond and Martha Titus helped establish the town of Westbury in 1671 along with local Quaker Henry Willis. Both families were active in the Society of Friends. It was in fact a formative time for the Quaker faith in America. George Fox, the English founder of Quakerism, toured and preached all over Long Island from 1671 to 1673. Edmond Titus held Quaker meetings in his house in Westbury just as his sister-in-law Mary Washburne Willets did in Jericho. Persecution of Quakers was still common in these early years, because they refused to pay support for the Dutch ministers—whose churches they did not attend—and they were fined for holding their own meetings for worship.

Edmond and Martha Titus prospered and had eleven children. A daughter, Martha, married Benjamin Seaman, son of Captain John Seaman, and a son Peter Titus married Martha Jackson, daughter of John Jackson.

Willet Titus, a descendant of the Westbury family, born in 1870, married Harriet Burt Hegeman and moved to Jericho. Their son Burt Titus was born in Jericho and lived on a portion of the family farm with his wife Marguerite until his death in 2002. Their oldest son James and his wife Phyllis still live in Jericho with their two daughters, Jennifer and Amy. Their younger son, Peter, lives in Massachusetts with his family, and teaches at Massachusetts Institute of Technology. It is likely that Hegeman's Lane, Brookville, has a connection to this family, as certainly does Titus Path off Route 106.

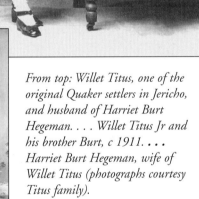

From top: Willet Titus, one of the original Quaker settlers in Jericho, and husband of Harriet Burt Hegeman. . . . Willet Titus Jr and his brother Burt, c 1911. . . . Harriet Burt Hegeman, wife of Willet Titus (photographs courtesy Titus family).

The Underhill Family

Captain John Underhill of Warwickshire, England, came to Boston in 1630. Hearing of his military prowess the Dutch invited him to come to New Amsterdam to help in local fighting, and his military successes brought heavy losses to the Native American population.

Caroline Underhill Jackson Hicks, youngest daughter of Solomon Seaman Jackson, was married on June 6, 1900, to Henry Hicks, son of Edward and Emma Hicks of Westbury (Esther Hicks Emory Collection, JPL Archives).

Captain John Underhill of Warwickshire, England, came to Boston in 1630.

Samuel Jackson Underhill, oldest son of Daniel and Caroline, married Emma Albertson and served as Supervisor of the Town of Oyster Bay from 1894-98. . . . Formal portrait of Hannah Underhill Hicks, daughter of Thomas and Sarah Underhill, and an early member of the Charity Society of Jericho and Westbury Monthly Meetings (photographs Underhill Collection, JPL Archives).

Daniel Underhill and Caroline Post Underhill, married at Westbury Meeting in 1847. After her death 35 years later, Daniel married her younger sister Catherine in 1883. . . . Daniel Underhill home with family on front porch, 1890s (photographs Underhill Collection, JPL Archives).

*Phebe Underhill Seaman
age 4, c 1901, in photograph by
"S. Young, located at 599 Fulton
Street, Brooklyn". . . . Phebe
Underhill Seaman as an adult,
1940s (photographs Tollaver
Collection, JPL Archives).*

The Underhill Farm, Jericho, L. I.

*Underhill barns in
Jericho, from an old
calendar painting of
Underhill Farm
(JPL Archives).*

*Phebe Underhill Seaman's
father Robert Seaman in his
easy chair, 1940s. The
Robert Seaman Elementary
School was named in his
honor (Tollaver Collection,
JPL Archives).*

Underhill bought a place in Southold in 1657, but soon received a land grant in Oyster Bay, and joined the Society of Friends. His great-great-great grandson, Daniel Underhill, married Mary Jackson in Jericho. Their son Adonijah married Phebe Hicks, a granddaughter of Elias Hicks. Phebe Underhill, daughter of Samuel J. and Mary Underhill, married Elias Hicks Seaman, son of Robert Seaman and Sarah Hicks. It is their granddaughter Phebe Underhill Seaman who in 1952 sold part of her property to developers, which contributed to the suburbanization of Jericho.

The Williams & Willets Families

Historic records confirm that Robert Williams, now familiar to us as the founder of Jericho, acquired his "Plantation" prior to May 20, 1648, the date of record for a deed entered in the "office of records at New Yorke." Williams was believed to have been a Quaker or at least had Quaker leanings. He and his wife Sarah Washburne had eight children—four boys and four girls. As mentioned, their son John married Oyster Bay resident Leah Townsend, and two of their daughters each married sons of Jonathan Seaman.

Sarah Washburne's sister Mary married Richard Willets, and after his death in about 1665, Oyster Bay records show that Williams deeded Mary about a third of his Jericho Plantation in 1667 and "she agreed to move there, with some of her children." The widow Mary Washburne Willets never remarried, but added on to her tiny little house next to the Spring Pond over the years. Influenced by her Quaker neighbors, Mary became a Quaker herself. Her son Richard and his wife Abigail Powell Willets were active Quakers. Mary opened her home to the Jericho Friends for Meeting for Worship, did some preaching herself and welcomed traveling Friends to spend the night in a quiet place, free of alcoholic spirits. By 1937 her modest home beside the Spring Pond evolved and expanded into a restaurant first called the Maine Maid Inn. Today it is well known as the Milleridge Inn Restaurant at the intersection of Jericho Turnpike at Route 106/107.

More about these two historic restaurants is found in Chapter 8.

So you see how many of the early families of Jericho were wonderfully—often confusingly!—interconnected.

So you see how many of the early families of Jericho were wonderfully—often confusingly!—interconnected. Still other Quaker and non-Quaker families were instrumental in the settlement and growth of Jericho. The family names Carll, Doughty, Ketcham, Malcolm, Townsend and Willets were later joined by Davis, Halleran, Tappan, Zulkofske and many more that have also played significant roles in Jericho's evolution. □

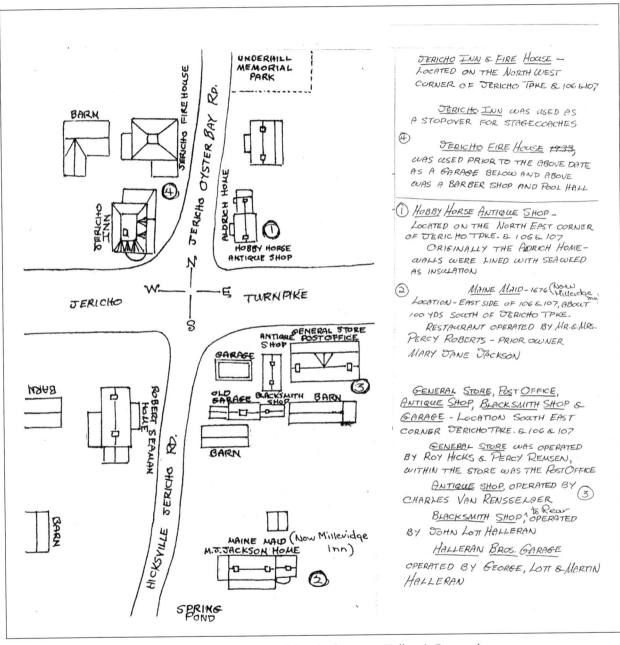

The map contains the following handwritten labels and annotations:

UNDERHILL MEMORIAL PARK

BARN

JERICHO FIRE HOUSE

JERICHO OYSTER BAY RD.

ALDRICH HOME

④

JERICHO INN

HOBBY HORSE ANTIQUE SHOP

①

W. — E.

N — S

JERICHO TURNPIKE

ANTIQUE SHOP

GENERAL STORE POST OFFICE

GARAGE

OLD GARAGE

BLACKSMITH SHOP

BARN

③

BARN

ROBERT SEAMAN HOME

BARN

HICKSVILLE JERICHO RD.

BARN

MAINE MAID (Now Millevidge Inn)
M.J. JACKSON HOME

②

SPRING POND

JERICHO INN & FIRE HOUSE —
LOCATED ON THE NORTH WEST
CORNER OF JERICHO TPKE. & 106 & 107

JERICHO INN WAS USED AS
A STOPOVER FOR STAGECOACHES

④ JERICHO FIRE HOUSE 1933,
WAS USED PRIOR TO THE ABOVE DATE
AS A GARAGE BELOW AND ABOVE
WAS A BARBER SHOP AND POOL HALL

① HOBBY HORSE ANTIQUE SHOP —
LOCATED ON THE NORTH EAST CORNER
OF JERICHO TPKE. & 106 & 107
ORIGINALLY THE ADRICH HOME —
WALLS WERE LINED WITH SEAWEED
AS INSULATION

② MAINE MAID — 1676 (Now Millevidge Inn)
LOCATION — EAST SIDE OF 106 & 107, ABOUT
100 YDS SOUTH OF JERICHO TPKE.
RESTAURANT OPERATED BY MR. & MRS.
PERCY ROBERTS — PRIOR OWNER
MARY JANE JACKSON

GENERAL STORE, POST OFFICE,
ANTIQUE SHOP, BLACKSMITH SHOP &
GARAGE — LOCATION SOUTH EAST
CORNER JERICHO TPKE. & 106 & 107

GENERAL STORE WAS OPERATED
BY ROY HICKS & PERCY REMSEN,
WITHIN THE STORE WAS THE POST OFFICE

ANTIQUE SHOP, OPERATED BY
CHARLES VAN RENSSELAER ③

BLACKSMITH SHOP, to Rear OPERATED
BY JOHN LOTT HALLERAN

HALLERAN BROS. GARAGE
OPERATED BY GEORGE, LOTT & MARTIN
HALLERAN

Annotated hand-drawn map shows Jericho Corners—with keyed references to Halleran's Garage, the General Store serving also as Post Office, and other familiar businesses and homes— before construction of 1950s cloverleaf (Marty Halleran Collection, JPL Archives).

*Long Island was an occupied territory
for seven tumultuous years, until 1783.*

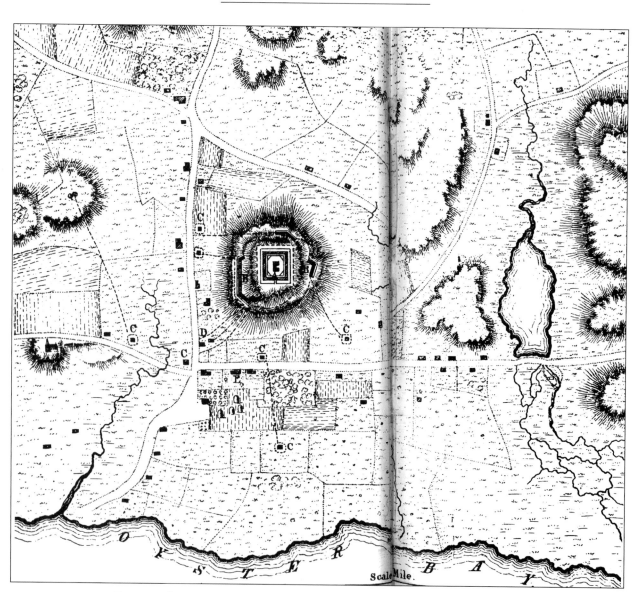

Drawing of Oyster Bay revolutionary fortification attributed to Lt. Col. Simcoe (from McGee, Sally
Townsend, Patriot; *JPL Archives).*

JERICHO &
THE AMERICAN REVOLUTION 6

I know that there were some British troops quartered in Jericho
during the Revolutionary War and there was a small fort there. But, I understand
that it didn't last very long. I believe they called it "Fort Nonsense" because the
local people felt it was not necessary.

— Oral history transcript of George Doughty,
Jericho resident and owner of the Jericho Cider Mill, 1975

The legendary French and Indian Wars (1744-63) were a colossal expense for the English monarchy. At this time the colonists were still loyal to the Crown, so the New York Colony sent £150,000 to England to help pay for the war—and contributed their required quota of men to the British army as well. To ease its financial troubles further, Parliament passed laws to increase its control over the colonies, and to make the colonists pay for maintaining a permanent standing army on their side of the ocean.

For twelve long years the colonists, accustomed to more self-government than the new laws allowed, argued against the new policies and the heavy taxes levied upon them—including the Sugar Act of 1764, the famed Stamp Act of 1766 and the Townsend duties of 1767. Boycotts and riots led to violence in several cities. Matters were additionally strained with the passing of the Quartering or Billeting Act, which allowed any overflow of British troops to be given shelter in public inns and in private barns or homes.

As is well known, the ensuing Boston Tea Party in 1773 led to the battle at Lexington and marked the beginning of the eight-year war for American independence. A group of leading Patriots banded together in 1774 and set up a Continental Congress. The Congress passed an embargo on British goods, issued a Declaration of Rights and named George Washington commander of their newly formed Continental Army. Enlistments were ordered and personal weapons were confiscated to arm the new colonial military. But an angry British Parliament soon declared the Massachusetts Colony to be in "rebellion" and ordered British troops to take military action in Boston.

Colonial issues were not as clear cut on Long Island, however, as they were in New England. After the news from Lexington reached the colonists out on the eastern end of Long Island, they sided immediately with their close neighbors in New England. But apparently the Dutch, Walloon, Swedish and other nationalities in New York and Brooklyn didn't really care who was in control as long as they could live in peace and prosperity. It was Queens County (which at that time included today's Nassau County and thus Jericho) that had the most divided population.

The Dutch settlers in Queens had no love for the English, but along with wealthy English colonists on the South Shore they felt war could mean a possible loss of money, time, property and their own personal comfort. Many colonists had lucrative business dealings with England. Others were opposed to getting involved in any activity that might be considered illegal, or treasonous to their king. Questioning the authority of the Crown went against their deep-rooted feelings of social and civic responsibility.

Most anti-Crown Patriots lived along the North Shore. Great Neck, Cow Neck (now Port Washington) and Hempstead Harbor actually seceded from the Tory (Loyalist) township of Hempstead in October of 1775. Yet another population segment in the very same neighborhoods was ardently Tory, sometimes to the horror of their families and friends.

Local accounts show that the large Quaker population on the Island—including Jericho and Westbury—was opposed to any form of warfare for any cause at all. All people, of every persuasion, were shocked when violence did erupt. Looting, destruction of Loyalist property, confiscation of goods and even imprisonment soon became commonplace. By August 1776 there were nearly five hundred British warships with an impressive forty thousand troops at anchor in New York Harbor. The Continental Congress had formed militias without delay, but a mere twenty thousand untrained Patriots were up against twice as many seasoned British and Hessian troops who landed on western Long Island on August 22, 1776.

Officer of the Loyalist Queen's Rangers—a regiment that served in Jericho (courtesy Company of Military Historians, from Military Uniforms in America). *. . . Map of the Battle of Long Island, August 27, 1776, showing engagements of British and American armies (from* A Tour Around New York, *John Mines, 1893).*

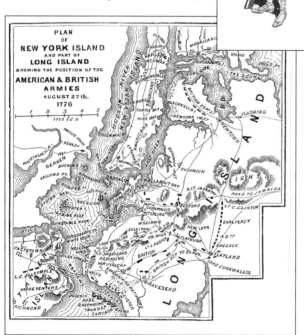

The Battle of Long Island—which took place in Brooklyn no more than thirty miles from Jericho—nearly marked the end of the Patriot cause. Their commander General George Washington ordered his defeated forces to retreat from Brooklyn when they were outflanked and nearly overwhelmed by the British moving up from Gravesend through the Jamaica Pass. All through the night, under cover of dense fog, the surviving Patriot troops were ferried across the East River to Manhattan and safety. As history books are proud to say, this brilliant move made a hero out of George Washington and saved his men to fight another day.

Long Island was an occupied territory for seven tumultuous years, until 1783. Martial law was imposed and traditional justice suspended. Loyalist farmers were oftentimes treated no better than the Patriots, with towns, farms, homes and churches plundered no matter which side they supported; it was a terrible time for all. Many Long Island Patriot husbands and sons had already fled to Connecticut to serve in the Continental Army, leaving their women and children behind to deal with the farms, the animals and the occupying British troops.

Some stories say that Hessian and British troops built barracks in Jericho. "Fort Nonsense" was reputed to have been built on a hill "around Townsend's barn," now Underhill property. In the 1960s, staff from the Nassau County Museum investigated the area where the fort was supposed have been located but found no evidence of its existence, despite the locals who believe it to be true.

British troops were also quartered in private homes in and around Jericho, especially in the winter. They camped on farmlands as well. A page from the notebook of a British Quartermaster records who stayed where and how much money was supposedly paid to the homeowners. Elias and Jemima Hicks, for example, had to give space for "1 Judge Advocate," and another Jericho resident, Zebulon Williams, had to take in eighteen men for "1 pound 7 shillings, for 1-1/2 rooms."

QUEENS COUNTY—2D SERIES. 19

1780, March 22. This certifies that Obadiah Platt's wagon and horses have been employed three days to carry the baggage of the Prince of Wales' American Regiment from Lloyd's Neck to Flushing Fly.
JOHN CARDEN,* Major.

1780, July 23. Received of P. Smith, for the use of Capt. Whitehead's troop of Light Dragoons, on His Majesty's service, two bushels Indian corn and eighteen meals of victuals.
CORNELIUS RAPELYE,
Qr. Mas., Q. Co. M.

1780, July 31. Received of John Ketcham rations for fourteen horses, one day, of Capt. Hewlett's troop of Queens County Militia.
STEPHEN HEWLETT,
Captain Q. Co. M.

1780, Aug. 21. Huntington South. Received from George Norton 120 lbs. oats, for the use of my troops on duty to the east part of Long Island, commanded by Col. Simcoe. Never paid for.
STEPHEN HEWLETT, Captain.

1780, Sept. 23. Jamaica. I certify that eight wagons (four ox-teams) were employed two days in carrying the sick of the 2d Battalion Light Infantry from Huntington to Jamaica.   THOMAS ARMSTRONG, Maj. Com't.
R. ABERCROMBIE, 1st Capt.

1780, Nov. 21. N. H. carted hay to Herricks.

1780, Dec. Capt. Israel Youngs, Deputy Superintendent of Forage, took a load of salt hay from Joseph White ; Nov. 21, he took a load of English hay.

1781, June. When Colonel Ludlow left Lloyd's Neck, Captain Lester prest horses, wagon and driver from John Buffit, to carry the baggage to Flushing.

1781, Nov. 12. Cold Spring. Received of Richard Conklin fourteen rations of hay for the use of the Queens County Brigade horses now employed carting forage for the Commissary General.
ISAAC YOUNGS, Supt. of Forage.
To GEORGE BRINLEY, Esq.

1781, Dec. 10. To John Hewlett, Superintendent of Forage. I certify that there have been eight horses of the Queens County Brigade (now employed carting forage for the Commanding General) rationed one night on English hay belonging to Samuel Lewis.
PETER WALTERS.

* Carden died at Charleston, 1782.

1782, Feb. 6. I certify that seventeen horses of the Queens County Brigade, now employed carting forage for the Commissary General, have been rationed one night on salt hay of D. Rusco.
JOHN HEWLETT, Supt. of Forage.
To GEORGE BRINLEY.

1783, Feb. 21. East Woods. This is to certify that Jasper Kellum brought a load of baggage for the Corps of Guides and Pioneers from Long Swamp to East Woods, six miles.
JONATHAN WILLIAMS, Captain.

COLONEL TARLTON AT JERICHO.

1777, Nov. Zophar Platt was prest, with his ox-team, by Major Cochran, to carry a load of boards to Tarlton's quarters at Jericho. He also took forty pounds of butter, without giving a receipt or pay. Job Sammis was employed one day in carting poultry to Jericho by Tarlton's orders.

1778, Nov. 24. Lieut.-Col. Cochran took from Henry Smith six geese and two dozen fowls and twenty pounds of butter, and from E. Gillet a cheese and fourteen pounds of butter.

1778, Dec. 10. Quartermaster Davis took 504 feet of boards from Solomon Ketcham and 400 feet from S. Sammis, and carted them to Jericho.

1778, Dec. 23. Tarlton's troops, on their march from Smithtown to Jericho, took four fat hogs from Jeremiah Ruland and three from Zebulon Buffet. Daniel Blatchly had bought five dozen and ten fowls to carry to New York market for Christmas. They were taken from him by Tarlton's orders, also two barrels of cider.

1779, Oct. 7. Received of James Oakley a small heifer of 248 pounds weight, for the use of the sick of the Provincial cavalry.
JOHN TUCK, Qr. Mas. Brit. Legion.
BANASTRE TARLTON, Lt. Col.

1779, Oct. 20. Tarlton, being out on a party of pleasure and grousing, came to Timothy Carll's house and in person took a cow out of his pasture and killed her for his troops. No pay.

1780, March 5. Received of Nehemiah Whitman five bushels oats for the use of the 2d Battalion Jersey Volunteers stationed at Jericho.
GEO. LAMBERT, Lt. & acting Qr. Mas.
JOHN COLDEN, 2d Major.

Revolutionary Incidents text from Henry Onderdonk Jr's book details small but fascinating Revolutionary events, among them Col. Tarleton taking a cow from Timothy Carll's house and killing it for his troops (Onderdonk's Documents and Letters Intended to Illustrate the Revolutionary Incidents, *JPL Archives*).

Patriot families now suffered more than the Loyalists, though neither was spared the confiscation of goods, wagons and tools and the quartering of rowdy troops in their homes. Nor were the pacifist Quakers spared the cruelties of war. Their Flushing Meeting House, occupied for seven long years, was first used to quarter British troops, next as a prison, then a hospital and later a storehouse. These were challenging years.

The Quaker Yearly Meeting was held as usual at the Westbury Meeting House between 1778 and 1783 but with British soldiers camped in the yard. Some of the British soldiers even attended a Quaker Meeting for Worship from time to time. Unfortunately, the Oyster Bay Meeting House fared less well: it was occupied by the British and nearly demolished for firewood during the first winter, forcing the Quakers there to travel more than five miles south to worship with the Quakers in Jericho.

Lt. Col. John Graves Simcoe (1752-1806)—respected British officer commanding the American provincial Loyalist troops known as the Queen's Rangers—occupied and fortified Oyster Bay against the Patriots.

Quakers who refused to fight or assist the war effort were heavily fined and had many of their goods confiscated. If they did agree to cooperate, and used their wagons to haul military supplies as ordered, and if they paid the war taxes levied on them, they were liable to be "disowned" from their Meeting for going against the teaching of the Friends *Book of Discipline.*

On the other hand, Quakers in Jericho and elsewhere, being pacifists, found it easier to get passes to cross army lines to attend their Monthly and Yearly Meetings in New York City and Philadelphia, and even to visit other Friends—which was an important part of their lifestyle. They actively raised funds to be used to aid victims of the war, following a long tradition started in England that is still practiced by the Society of Friends today.

Documents are by no means complete, but do convey many other clear facts about the occupation years of 1776-83. For instance, Hessian mercenary troops were quartered in East Norwich, Cedar Swamp, Jericho and Westbury. A few attended the Dutch Reformed Church in Brookville, and quite a few remained on Long Island taking up residence in the Jericho–Westbury area after the war was over.

Lt. Col. Banastre Tarleton, who came from England with Cornwallis's troops to quell the colonial rebellion, was a dashing, young and brutal cavalryman nicknamed "Bloody Tarleton." He worked with Lt. Col. Simcoe and his Loyalist Queen's Rangers harassing the Americans.

Lieutenant Colonel John Graves Simcoe's personal journal—according to a reprinted copy in the JPL Archives—records that he marched his Loyalist cavalry troops to Jericho in 1778, where they remained under the command of his colleague Lieutenant Colonel Banastre Tarleton—noted in one biographical account as "the son of a wealthy Liverpool merchant" whose "successes in the New York, Philadelphia and Monmouth campaigns . . .

earned him the sobriquet 'Bloody Tarleton.'" Simcoe also writes that the Hussars of the Queen's Rangers, and a certain Captain Sandford's troops, were later transferred from Jericho to Staten Island. An advertisement posted in the area asked local men to join the British army, citing: for "good pay, clothing and provision regular . . . apply to Cap't Henry Seton, at Huntington, Oyster Bay and Jericho, who gives £5 over and above the King's bounty. GOD save the KING."

M ost fighting ceased on Long Island in 1781, but peace wasn't official for another two years. In Jericho as elsewhere, reprisals against the Loyalists were now so intense that many suffering families were forced to leave Long Island for good. Their civil rights were lost, their lands and businesses forfeited. Some even had prices on their heads. When the British and Hessian troops finally departed from New York City, thousands of Loyalists from New York and Long Island went with them, bound for the West Indies, England or Canada where the British government granted them land. Many Quakers also left Long Island to seek peace in Canada. Family records show that even several members of the Hicks family from Jericho and Westbury sought a new life in Canada. □

GOOD PAY, CLOTHING AND PROVISION REGULAR APPLY to CAPT HENRY SETON at HUNTINGTON, OYSTER BAY and JERICHO WHO GIVES £5 OVER and ABOVE the KING'S BOUNTY GOD SAVE THE KING

Invitation to join the British army.

Elias Hicks

The famed Elias Hicks in an undated portrait (JPL Archives).
. . . Hand-drawn map of Jericho, "home of Elias Hicks from 1771
to 1830," showing site of Spring Pond, Friends Meeting House, and
Jericho Turnpike running horizontally east to west (from Forbush's
Hicks, Quaker Liberal).

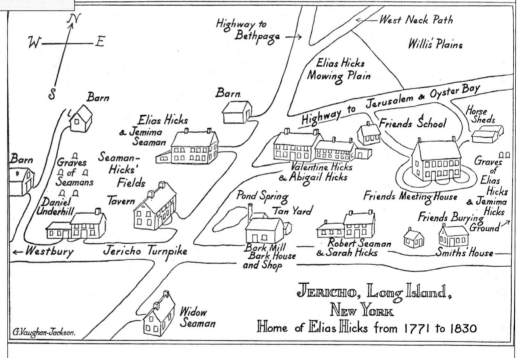

Elias Hicks
– Quaker Preacher

7

I was born on the 19th day of the third month, 1748, in the township of Hempstead, in Queens county, on Long Island. My parents, John and Martha Hicks, were descended from reputable families, and sustained a good character among their friends and those who knew them. My father was a grandson of Thomas Hicks, of whom our worthy friend Samuel Bownes makes honorable mention in his journal. . . . Neither of my parents were members in strict fellowship with any religious society until some time before my birth. My father at that period was united in membership with Friends. . . .

—Elias Hicks, *The Journal of Elias Hicks, 1832*

Elias Hicks was the fourth of six sons born to the professed Quaker John Hicks and his wife Martha, who lived in Hempstead and later in Rockaway. Historian Bliss Forbush's 1956 biography of Elias Hicks tells us that his Anglican grandfather, Jacob Hicks, was very impressed by a traveling Quaker preacher, and allowed him to use the Hicks's home for "monthly gatherings for worship" by the controversial Religious Society of Friends. Elias's father John was so moved by the faith of these Friends that he became a convert, and registered with the Westbury Meeting.

This means Elias was born a Quaker, a birthright member of the Meeting, as compared to a "convinced" member, or convert. The Hicks family attended Meeting together, where Elias reported that he felt "divine grace."

Like many youngsters of this time, Elias received irregular schooling, but did very well in reading and writing. He also had to learn all the jobs of a typical farmer—plowing, harvesting, grinding flour, butchering, smoking and pickling among them.

Whenever possible, Forbush tells us, Elias liked to go hunting, fishing and clamming off the shores of Rockaway, and he learned to salt and dry the fish he caught in the inlets. His mother Martha died when Elias was eleven. A few years later his father sent him to live in another town with Samuel, an older married brother. While living there he learned to play games and cards, race horses and dance at country balls. He was apprenticed to an itinerant carpenter at age seventeen, and traveled from one place to another as he learned the trade. Forbush's biography tells us that Elias also indulged in "other frivolous and vain amusements," such as dancing and horseracing.

After years of apparent indifference to his faith, Elias's thoughts and mode of life changed. He spent some of his leisure time reading the Scriptures and soon found his interests changed to less worldly pursuits. As his carpentry apprenticeship finished, he spent less time with his former acquaintances and more time with members of the Religious Society of Friends. He began to meditate, attend Quaker Meetings and generally become a more devout person.

When he returned home to his father and stepmother, Phebe Powell, he attended the Westbury Meeting, where he met and became interested in a young Quaker girl, Jemima Seaman of Jericho. Elias and Jemima began their courting by attending Meetings together all over the area, at Cow Neck/Manhasset, Bethpage and Matinecock, as well as their own Meeting at Westbury. This gave them time to spend alone with each other, and eventually Elias was invited to visit the Seaman homestead on today's Old Jericho Turnpike.

Elias married Jemima in 1771, at age twenty-two, at the Westbury Meeting. Their marriage certificate was signed and witnessed, in the Quaker custom, by the elders and members of the Meeting. After a few months in Rockaway, the young couple was invited to move into the Seaman home in Jericho with Jemima's parents and grandparents. Her brothers had all died young so Elias and Jemima were needed to help with the work, both indoors and out.

Forbush's research confirms that the couple proclaimed their belief in the Quaker virtue of industry, and their personal accountability to God for the best use of their time on earth. They believed that a tidy and prosperous farm with full barns, healthy animals, a weather-proof house and a full pantry would give them peace of mind, and the freedom to pray. Each season on the Seaman farm, flax was raised and spun into cloth, as was the wool shorn from their sheep. Shoes for the family, and harnesses for the horses, were made from the hides of their cattle and tanned in the Seaman family's own tannery. Pillows were stuffed with down and feathers from their ducks, and wood for fence posts and tools was cut from their woodland. They prospered, and in the Quaker tradition, frequently shared their surpluses with anyone in need. Elias also learned the practice of surveying, which he was able to put to use on the surrounding farms in Jericho.

By age twenty-six Elias had undergone a fervent spiritual renewal and rededicated himself to all the practices of the Society of Friends.

Elias led an exceedingly busy life! He helped run the Seaman farm and tannery. He attended both First and Fourth Day Meetings for Worship at Monthly Meeting in Westbury, and the Yearly Meeting in Flushing. As early as 1775, more than eighty years before the Civil War, he became heavily involved in the fight for the abolition of slavery among Quakers, following the Quaker belief that *all* people are equal in the eyes of God.

In 1776, Elias was appointed to be one of a committee that visited local Friends who owned slaves to "discourage . . . the further purchase of Negroes," and encourage manumission of those they already owned. He was reluctant to do this at first. Yet within a year, thanks in large measure to Elias's efforts, more than eighty-five slaves were manumitted by members of the Westbury Meeting.

It was certainly a challenging year for these efforts: the American Revolution was being waged in many Long Island towns and villages. As mentioned, British troops commandeered every possible public building, church and Quaker Meeting house. They used the

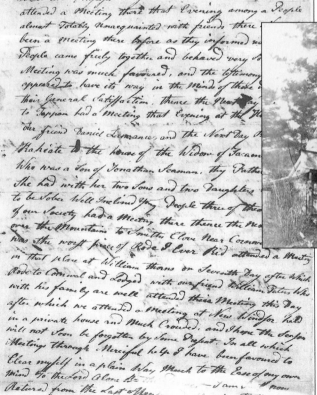

Letter from Elias Hicks to his wife Jemima, 1791, concerning his trip to New Jersey and New York. "Beloved Wife—Having but little time to write these may inform thee that after leaving Rahway we attended a Meeting at Elizabeth Town . . ." Seaman/Hicks House (Esther Hicks Emery Collection, JPL Archives).

Elias married Jemima in 1771, at age twenty-two, at the Westbury Meeting.

buildings as their headquarters, their warehouses and even as their prisons or stables. The Quakers suffered intensely because of their pacifist neutrality. They were distrusted by both sides, and many fled to Canada to avoid the war.

Elias Hicks continued to grow in influence in the Society of Friends. His firm stand against the evils of war and for the cause of peace, along with his constant struggle to abolish slavery, fueled his effort to make his fellow Quakers free their slaves. By 1791, with his ardent appeals, the Westbury Meeting's total number of manumissions would rise to one hundred fifty-four.

Elias had been appointed to the Preparative Meeting of Ministers and Elders in 1778. Now a recorded preacher in the Society of Friends, he dedicated himself to spreading the gospel of truth. At the same time he continued to carry out his worldly responsibilities and labors of everyday life. On the road again in 1779 he attended the Yearly Meetings in New York, Westchester and Philadelphia.

It was in early 1787 that the Jericho Friends petitioned Westbury Meeting for permission to establish their own Meeting. With permission granted, the members purchased, for £45, more than an acre of land from the Wright family on the east side of Oyster Bay Road—today Route 106—just north of Jericho Turnpike, for the new Meeting House. Hicks surveyed the land and, local records suggest, probably designed the building. A committee was appointed to oversee the project: a cedar shingled square structure with shuttered windows, finished sometime in 1788. A porch was added later in 1818 in traditional Meeting House style, and Jericho Meeting House is still in active use two centuries later.

Royal Aldrich home, built by Elias Hicks just south of his own, when Royal married his daughter Martha. When Jericho Turnpike was moved southward in 1929 the home became the Hobby Horse Antique Shop; it was demolished for cloverleaf construction, 1950s (James Abbe photograph, JPL Archives).

The Jericho Meeting had grown steadily from its inception, even though as many members joined, others were disowned for not keeping to the rules of the Quaker *Book of Discipline.* As firm believers in education, the Quakers soon appointed a committee to build a school on the property. Completed in 1793, the school building survives today as the caretaker's cottage at the Jericho Meeting House.

In 1793, Jemima herself was appointed to the Ministers and Elders, and gave birth to her tenth child, although only five were still living. Their daughter Martha had married Royal Aldrich the year before and moved into a house, just south of her parents, that Elias gave them. David, their eldest, had died in 1787, the same month their last son, John, was born. Dr. Mary M. Mass writes in her dissertation on the Hicks family that Elias's journal describes all his sons as healthy to the age of ten. She deduces that they were stricken with a disease such as muscular dystrophy after that age, but a sad mystery still surrounds the tragic deaths.

Elias remained at home for three years with his family before resuming his ministry travels. He had stayed in Jericho to comfort his wife, to deal with affairs at home—and even to fill in as teacher at the Friends school when a hired schoolmaster could not be found.

Continuing his fight to abolish slavery, Elias strongly urged a boycott of all slave-produced goods such as rice, cotton and sugar. He dedicated himself to improving the conditions of local freed blacks through the Quakers' Charity Society—founded in 1794 and still active today after more than two centuries of charitable efforts, primarily for children.

In 1810—still a half century before the Civil War and the Emancipation Proclamation, and after the Yearly Meeting failed to take a firm enough stand against slavery to suit him— Elias wrote a twenty-four-page pamphlet condemning slavery and the use of all goods produced by slave labor. The pamphlet continued to be so effective that it caused strong sentiments, both pro and con on the subject, as far away as England.

Continuing his fight to abolish slavery, Elias strongly urged a boycott of all slave-produced goods such as rice, cotton and sugar.

Most slave owners were afraid that manumission would lead to economic ruin. In his travels, Hicks spoke with such intense conviction that his sermons lasted anywhere from a half hour to two hours. They were written in shorthand and transcribed by a Mr. M. T. C. Gould. Printed copies can still be read today in the JPL archives. In one stretch of years, 1812-15, he traveled more than two thousand miles by horse and buggy through New Jersey, Pennsylvania and Maryland, preaching his anti-slavery convictions. Slavery would finally end in Jericho soon thereafter in 1817, when the last slave was freed.

In his sixties, Elias Hicks continued to work at home, to preach and to teach. He still traveled for months at a time by buggy and horseback preaching to all who would listen. Elias's cousin Isaac Hicks, a wealthy ship owner in New York, returned to live in Westbury, and accompanied Elias on many of these preaching trips. Isaac's son and business partner Valentine, who was married to Elias's daughter Abigail, bought the Tredwell house in Jericho in 1814, and moved in across the road from her parents. Their home is the core of the Maine Maid Inn today. That same year, Abigail's sister Sarah married Robert Seaman; they moved into the house on Jericho Turnpike that Elias had built for them, and Robert helped Elias with the tannery.

Four years later, at the age of seventy, Elias was back on the road again traveling, but the Society of Friends would soon enter a period of crisis. There was a conflict of doctrine in the annual "Epistle" sent from the Friends in England. Several different doctrines were being preached in the New York Yearly Meeting, and some Quakers felt there was a need for a definite, or orthodox, creed to be followed by all Quakers. Hicks spoke out against this plan with great eloquence. His ban of all slave products, and certain other of his "testimonies," caused some Friends to question his views. Elias stood firm in his beliefs and continued his opposition to the champions of capitalism, and his fight for liberty, brotherly love and the need to follow the "true light."

Sectionalism and democracy swept the country in 1827. Andrew Jackson was elected president—one of the few early presidents not born of an aristocratic or wealthy family. The Friends Yearly Meetings were now full of conflicts and the Society split into different orthodox and liberal groups. Elias Hicks set out on yet another religious mission through Ohio, Indiana, Virginia, Maryland and Pennsylvania. Other Quaker preachers followed a similar route and attacked his teachings. Hicks was banned from some Meetings and welcomed in others. This schism of the Orthodox and the "Hicksite" Quakers would cause a rift in the Society of Friends that lasted for over 125 years until 1955, when they finally reunited.

Hicks continued his lengthy mission and didn't return home for seven months and ten days. This time he had traveled over 2,400 miles, and he was now eighty years old. In 1828, Jemima and his youngest daughter Elizabeth went into New York City to welcome him home. He remained with them in Jericho, and dealt with his affairs much as he had before.

Early in the spring of 1829, Jemima died of pneumonia in the house where she had been born seventy-eight years before. Always an affectionate husband, Elias spoke of his "dear departed companion" at her funeral. He wrote in his journal of his grief and "irreparable loss" of his wife of fifty-eight years, as he listed her death below the record of the deaths of seven of their children. He sold forty of his seventy-five acres to his son-in-law Valentine Hicks to ease some of his burdens and to have more time and energy to devote to his religious works. The aged preacher still felt his own duties were not fully discharged.

Gravestones of Elias and Jemima Hicks in the Jericho Meeting Burying Ground (Abbe Collection, JPL Archives).

Elias attended the New York Yearly Meeting in 1829, preaching against the construction of the Erie Canal and the development of the Baltimore and Ohio Railroad as being dangers to the "plain" religious life. He feared too much modern progress and worldly exposure wasn't good for Quakers. He undertook still another journey of 1,500 miles around Lake Champlain and down the Hudson Valley, preaching to Hicksite Quakers and to anyone else who would listen.

That winter he suffered a stroke after riding to Islip to visit his daughter Phebe Hicks Willets. Elias Hicks died following a second stroke on February 27, 1830. He was eighty-two years old. He was buried next to Jemima and his children in the Quaker Burying Ground at the Jericho Meeting House, where their tombstones can still be seen today.

A few days after his death, among the spontaneous outburst of tributes came a particularly moving one from the African Benevolent Society of New York, honoring him for his "indefatigable exertions" in his heroic fight for the abolition of slavery still decades before the Emancipation Proclamation, the end of the Civil War, and enactment of the Thirteenth Amendment in late 1865. ☐

Elias Hicks & the Quaker Faith

- The Quaker guideline to "Christian ethics" encompassed both *The Book of Discipline* and the writings of George Fox, the English founder of the Society of Friends. Meetings had no paid clergy or leadership, but Ministers and Overseers were appointed to conduct the Business Meeting (later called the Select Meeting) for the flock. Any member of the congregation, male or female, had an equal opportunity to speak during the Meetings for Worship if they were so inspired "by Divine revelation and knowledge." Those who felt a very strong inner calling to ministry or preaching were welcome to share their "inner light" with fellow Friends. Quakers were totally opposed to hired, or paid, preachers or clergy, believing it was wicked to accept money for preaching the Word of God.

- Quakers in the Hicksite tradition have no ministers, prayer books or doctrines, but follow the principles in a document called "The Advices and Queries" which are read monthly at Meeting for Worship. Meetings are for silent contemplation with occasional verbal sharing of joys, concerns or experiences by the congregation if they are so moved. The Meetings close with all shaking hands.

- During the American Revolution, Quakers who refused to pay a tax when they were exempted from service were fined, sometimes imprisoned, and often had money, tools, other personal goods and livestock confiscated. If a Quaker cooperated with the armies of either side, however, he might be disciplined or even "disowned" from membership in the Meeting.

- Hicks was recognized as one of the most convincing Quaker preachers of his period, and in 1813 he began to keep a "home journal." This type of journal, usually written by itinerant preachers, was popular reading material for young Friends, whose choice of acceptable reading materials was limited. These Quaker journals were the equivalent of adventure tales, and were welcomed by Meeting members as models for a proper Quaker lifestyle for young readers. They were also used as a means of introducing the faith to outsiders. Hicks dedicated a specific period of time in each day for quiet meditation and spiritual exercises.

- Hicks firmly shared the Quaker belief in the "Inner Light," a directive from God, as the primary authority for a person's life. He believed that all other authorities, including the Bible, were secondary because the scriptures were written by mortal men and could be fallible, and he rejected the concept of "original sin."

- Of the 223 members of the Jericho Meeting, 211 sided with Hicks, nine withdrew and three remained neutral. In the New York, Philadelphia and Baltimore Meetings the "Hicksites" were in the majority, but the Ohio Meeting was equally divided.

- There are hints of participation by members of the Hicks families in Westbury and Jericho in the Underground Railroad. The need for secrecy in this clandestine activity makes evidence scarce, even in family records.

- The Society of Friends displayed great missionary zeal and was active on Long Island for many years. Although the number of Quakers has diminished, today there are still seven active meetings, which are part of the Long Island Quarterly Meeting. They all are united in their quest for promoting peace, equality and care for the earth.

Milleridge Inn when it was a private home, occupied by the Jacksons in the 1920s (Doughty Collection, JPL Archives). . . . Menu cover from the new Maine Maid Inn, c 1970 (JPL Archives).

Maine Maid Inn seen on an old postcard sketch, from its years south of Jericho Turnpike where the Milleridge Inn is today, with Spring Pond shown here in foreground (Florence Bates Tollaver Collection, JPL Archives).

THE MAINE MAID
& MILLERIDGE INNS 8

Q: You mentioned that the teachers stayed at the Milleridge. Did they stay with a family?
A: I believe it was the Willets' home then [1800s] and later [c 1930]
it was the Jacksons'. The teachers . . . boarded at this home.
—Oral history transcript of Margaret Hartigan Wolf,
Jericho resident and teacher, 1977

Q: [Tell me about the Inns—the Maine Maid and the Milleridge.]
A: Originally the Milleridge Inn was [called] the Maine Maid Inn.
I worked there when I was 16, 17 and 18 [1940s]
at the Maine Maid under Mr. and Mrs. [Percy] Roberts.
Q: What was your position?
A: When I first worked there I made butter balls . . . we had paddles and
we used to take the butter and roll it. When she [Mrs. Roberts]
wasn't looking we used to flip them. We did! . . . then I became a "Pot Pie Girl."
We went around with chicken pot pies and Boston baked
beans (on a tray). . . and the customers would take it [from us].
—Oral history transcript of Philomena Wysolovski,
Jericho resident, 2001

It was in about 1672 that Mary Washburne Willets, previously introduced as the widow of Richard Willets and a sister-in-law of Robert
Williams, moved into a newly built tiny two-room house with a central
fireplace, near a natural spring pond at the crossroads of the
"Hicksville–Oyster Bay Road" and the "Jericho Road" (today's Route
106/107 and Jericho Turnpike). Mary's son Richard Jr rebuilt the central
part of the house in 1686. (These rooms and fireplace may still be seen
today in their nearly original condition just inside the main entrance of
the Milleridge Inn.) The Willets House upper story would be added nearly two centuries
later, in 1880. When Richard Jr. died in 1703 his widow Abigail remained with her mother-
in-law, "in their long continued widowhood." The house was added onto again and again
until it became a large, gracious home.

The small Quaker community flourished and grew around what everyone referred to as the "Spring Pond." Mary Washburne Willets became a convinced Quaker and held Meetings for Worship in her home. Often she offered exhausted travelers a quiet, safe and alcohol-free meal and place to spend the night.

The practice of quartering British and Hessian troops in the colonists' homes was, as mentioned, a major cause of friction in the occupation years 1776-83. Local records show that many of them were quartered in Jericho—sometimes in the homes of Mary Washburne Willets and Elias Hicks. When peace and prosperity finally returned in 1783, the residents of Jericho found that their little crossroads on the turnpike had developed into an important stopover for weary horse and wagon travelers. To prevent taverns and alehouses from coming to the Jericho settlement, the Willets, Hicks and other Quaker families opened their homes to travelers and gave them a meal and a place by the hearth to sleep. Stews, roasts and bread might be offered for nourishment. The Quaker families refused offers of payment, but the host and hostess often found coins after their guests had left.

The Jericho Turnpike Company was formed on March 20, 1813, in response to increased need for a proper road. The Company improved the turnpike surface, but charged a toll to use the road. Traffic past the crossroads was busy, for it was a major route into New York City for farmers, traders and traveling businessmen.

Mary Washburne Willets's now spacious house—enjoyed by Long Islanders today as the Milleridge Inn—was handed down from generation to generation to assorted descendants who carried the names Willets, Willis, Seaman, Hicks and Jackson. It remained a private

Postcard view of Valentine Hicks House, now Maine Maid Inn, 1950s (JPL Archives).

home, though it was occasionally rented out to families such as the Benjamin Doughtys—the Quaker family that bought the Ketcham & Jagger Cider Mill on the Oyster Bay Road in about 1890. Benjamin George Doughty was a skilled photographer who took pictures of old Jericho with a camera that used glass plate negatives. Fortunately for us all, the fragile glass plates were donated to the Jericho Public Library archives in the mid-1970s and remain a valuable part of the Library's collection. Benjamin Doughty's son George tells us the family lived in the Mary Washburne Willets house briefly until their new home was built on the Oyster Bay Road (Route 106), where it still stands today.

In 1937 the Willets house, with all its extensions, was leased to the Percy L. Roberts family of Sea Cliff. They converted the building into a restaurant and named it the Maine Maid Inn—Mrs. Roberts was born in Maine, and that had been the name of their former restaurant in Sea Cliff. Being Quakers they served simple "homemade" food, and did not serve any liquor. The hostesses dressed in colonial costumes reminiscent of the building's early days. It was a popular family place to eat.

The Maine Maid became the Milleridge Inn in the 1950s, shown here with the Spring Pond (at left and below), fondly called "the duck pond." Within a decade the pond was filled during the cloverleaf construction (Braner Collection, JPL Archives; Milleridge Collection, JPL Archives).

The Mary Washburne Willets house itself, the former Maine Maid Inn on the Spring Pond, reopened a few years later as the "Mille Ridge Restaurant."

Milleridge Village, 1979 (Engel Collection, JPL Archives). . . . Milleridge Inn signpost, late 1950s (Braner Collection, JPL Archives).

Valentine Hicks home, c 1850, almost a century before it became the Maine Maid Inn (JPL Archives).

. . . the residents of Jericho found that their little crossroads on the turnpike had developed into an important stopover for weary horse and wagon travelers.

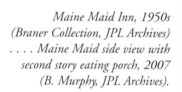

Maine Maid Inn, 1950s (Braner Collection, JPL Archives) . . . . Maine Maid side view with second story eating porch, 2007 (B. Murphy, JPL Archives).

Another notable Jericho house has an intriguing history as well. Around 1800, a man named Timothy Tredwell built a house across the Old Jericho Turnpike just east of the Seaman–Elias Hicks property, and a little south of the Malcolms' farm (today the Malcolm House and Barn). After Tredwell's death in 1814, Valentine Hicks, the cousin of Elias and a successful merchant and ship owner in New York City, bought the house and moved into it with his wife Abigail and three daughters. Valentine Hicks, who as mentioned was the second President of the Long Island Rail Road, was successful in getting the railroad extended out to a new eastern terminus—later named Hicksville in his honor. Valentine served as the Jericho Postmaster from 1826 to 1839, while the official local Post Office was—it is believed—located in the front room of his house. He died in 1850, but the house remained in private hands for the next hundred years.

It was in 1950 that the Roberts family failed in their attempt to purchase the Mary Washburne Willets house—which they had leased as home to their popular Maine Maid Inn restaurant for almost two decades. The Jacksons, who owned the building at that time didn't want to sell, so Roberts bought the former Valentine Hicks house from Mrs. Elvira Bayer on September 6, 1950. Percy and Lucille Roberts moved their Maine Maid Inn to its new location, where it remained until 2009, under new management as noted below, yet respecting the history and traditions of the old.

The Mary Washburne Willets house itself, the former Maine Maid Inn on the Spring Pond, reopened a few years later as the "Mille Ridge Restaurant." The quaint name refers to the natural stone ridge that skirted the old Spring Pond just south of the building. Before long a family from Texas, named Miller, purchased the "Mille Ridge" restaurant. The public misconceptions about spelling the restaurant's name all got resolved in 1961, when the Murphy family, of Murphy's Candlelight Restaurant fame, bought this restaurant and its ten-acre property. They restored the colonial atmosphere, added a "village" of shops and settled on the name Milleridge Inn. The Milleridge Cottage, a separate catering building for large parties and weddings, was added just east of the restaurant eight years later, in 1979. The Milleridge Inn still enjoys its popularity under the same family management today and this former Willets house can easily be seen by passersby at Route 106/107, just south of Jericho Turnpike.

. . . an alleged hiding place in the attic dating back to 19th century Underground Railroad days is a popular attraction.

Across the Turnpike, in 1960-61, the Roberts family sold their second "Maine Maid Inn"—or the Valentine Hicks house as we know it—to John Donahue of Mainemaid Realty, Inc. Owned by several different corporations over the years, the Maine Maid Inn was run by David Huschle in 1963 and then by Philip Munson in 1979. Munson retired and sold the restaurant in 1998 to new owners Brian Kishner, Richard Gabby and Alex and Fred Hey. Next it was owned by the Lessing Corporation, and then, as owned by Payal and Rajiv Sharma, it was still a wonderfully popular restaurant that maintained its colonial atmosphere and family appeal. The back porch was enclosed in the 1950s for more dining space, and an alleged hiding place in the attic dating back to 19th century Underground Railroad days remains a popular attraction. □

Benjamin George Doughty (l) and friends on the porch of what is now the Milleridge Inn. The Doughty family lived here while their house was being built just north of the Cider Mill, where it still stands today (glass plate negative c 1890, Doughty Collection, JPL Archives).

In those early Jericho Cider Mill days, an old wooden screw-press mashed the apples, and the resulting cider was placed in barrels for fermenting.

Stately wooden Jericho Cider Mill apple barns stood on Route 106, and were moved eastward on the property when the road was widened in the 1950s (glass plate negative c 1890, Doughty Collection, JPL Archives).

THE TWO JERICHO CIDER MILLS 9

The cider mill was owned by Isaac Townsend Ketcham . . . apparently he had a partner, because some of the old records and some of the old bottles . . . indicated the company was known as Ketcham & Jagger. But, as far as I know, my grandfather bought the cider mill and the cider business from Isaac Ketcham back in the 1890s.
—Oral history transcript of George Doughty, former resident and Jericho Cider Mill owner, 1975

Aunt Margaret [Ketcham] (my father Isaac's sister) married William Jagger, a man quite different from the quiet family to which she belonged, but then Aunt Margaret was quite willing to step out of her home environment on occasion. The Jaggers had two daughters, Jane and Charity.
—Phebe Ketcham McAllister, in *Family Affairs or Going to Jericho,* 1939

Apple cider was a staple drink for families in the colonial days. It was cheap and available. Many farmers had apple trees and could make their own cider with a wooden hand press, but the first commercial cider mill in Jericho was the Ketcham & Jagger Cider Mill. Opened in the early 1800s, it was located on the Hicksville–Oyster Bay Road (Route 106), a little northwest of the present Jericho Cider Mill. It is not known if Ketcham and Jagger built the original mill and apple barns on that site or acquired them from a previous owner.

Ketcham and Jagger's mill, set on a sturdy rock and brick foundation, had a three-story wooden barn with the third floor used as a hayloft. Metal tracks in the basement—fragments still remain—most likely were used to push the carts full of apples into the mill and later to remove the large cider casks for shipment.

Russet apples were plentiful in 1800s North Shore Long Island. Despite being rather small, and not very pretty with a dull brownish skin, Russet apples have an intense flavor that makes an excellent cider. They still exist today but are rarely found in supermarkets or at farm stands.

In those early Jericho Cider Mill days, an old wooden screw-press mashed the apples, and the resulting cider was placed in barrels for fermenting. Next it was filtered using a secret process, bottled with the corks wired down the same way champagne is bottled—then aged in two large cave-like tunnels dug into the hillside behind the mill. The much-applauded end product was clear and sparkling, and tasted very much like French champagne. Bought not only by Long Islanders, it was shipped into New York City to fine restaurants, cafes and

Doughty family members pose on the porch: Benjamin G. Doughty's wife Adeliza Romer Lane Doughty is in the shawl. Louise Lott is seated with the ruffled dress in front with her daughter Marietta. Young George Bodine Doughty (lower r) was the last Doughty to own the Cider Mill, and sold it to John Zulkofske in 1938 (glass plate negative c 1890, Doughty Collection, JPL Archives).

Doughty homestead still stands atop a hill overlooking Route 106 (glass plate negative, circa 1890, Doughty Collection, JPL Archives).

Jericho Cider mill apple barns, 1950s, now owned by the Zulkofskes . . . Apple barns at the Jericho Cider Mill before being moved in late1950s (photographs Braner Collection, JPL Archives).

fancy grocery markets. Our early Jericho cider was so popular that it is rumored to have been shipped abroad.

It was about 1890, as mentioned, that Brooklyn resident and amateur photographer Benjamin George Doughty purchased the Ketcham & Jagger Cider Mill from Isaac Ketcham. William Jagger died on April 16 of that year. The mill was highly successful until 1919 when Prohibition decreed their sparkling champagne cider illegal. Regrettably, the secret filtering process died with Benjamin George Doughty in 1953.

Jericho's second cider mill opened in 1873, a thousand feet south of the first. It was owned and operated by John J. Hicks, a member of the extended Hicks family that lived in the area. The Hicks mill produced an apple cider vinegar and a sweet cider both made with a wooden hand press, and later a steam powered press. Harry Tappan, a grandson of John, inherited it after Hicks died in the early 1930s. He equipped the mill with a modern electric press in 1932.

When Tappan died in 1938, his cider mill was purchased by John Zulkofske, a farmer from Garden City who moved all of Tappan's mill equipment back up the road to the site of the original Ketcham & Jagger mill. Sadly, during the "improvement" of Route 106 and the construction of the cloverleaf in 1958-60, the old Ketcham & Jagger cider mill barns, which sat directly in the middle of what was to be the new road, were moved or demolished along with many other original Jericho buildings and homes.

Today's popular Jericho Cider Mill is located in a plain two-story white barn originally built about 1925 along Route 106. The mill now has an air-powered cider press and is operated by George, the son of John and Mary Zulkofske, along with his wife Agnes and their daughter Deborah. Apples for their cider now come from the Halsey orchards in the Mecox area near Bridgehampton, Long Island, and from orchards in the Hudson Valley as well. In the fall, the mill sells diverse varieties of fresh apples for eating and cooking, but most are used for producing three thousand gallons of fresh apple cider per day. Today cookies, cakes and pies are also for sale at our renowned Jericho Cider Mill, and in a selection of local stores. □

Jericho Cider Mill, 1940s, before being pivoted sideways to accommodate road construction . . . Apple crates pile up behind the Cider Mill, 1940s. The apples for Jericho cider are no longer grown in Jericho, but come in fresh from orchards out in eastern LI and upstate New York (photographs Zulkofske Collection, JPL Archives).

The General Store and Post Office c 1928. Located at the intersection of Jericho Turnpike and Routes 106-107, this was the last Post Office that had its home in a general store. The Post Office was relocated into its own building in 1960, next to Whole Foods Market on Broadway, when the old store was demolished for the notorious cloverleaf (JPL Archives). . . . The Mailman Cometh to Jericho—Jericho Post Office history by Linda Braner, published in 1960—yields reliable and intriguing Post Office background.

JERICHO POST OFFICE 10

When I was perhaps ten years old, I used to be asked to get the mail from the Post Office in the store opposite the hotel or to go there with a small basket of eggs to trade for something needed quickly—a bit of baking soda perhaps, or a loaf of bread. But we seldom bought bread in those days . . . nearly everything we used was homemade. Mail arrived about 11 o'clock and that made a hot walk home at that time in the summer. Father very often went himself.

—Caroline Jackson Hicks in her "Account of a Childhood in Jericho," 1931

Having to walk to and fro from the Post Office every day . . . I would walk up the Jericho Turnpike. There was a small stream flowing alongside the Turnpike and I would get to the corner and have to wait for the traffic, cross the traffic and then go to the grocery store. I picked up the mail, not only for myself but also for the neighbors. Before returning I would sit on the bench . . . and just take in the atmosphere of a true rural countryside.

—Oral history transcript of Linda Braner, author of *The Mailman Cometh*, 1975

As early as 1639, postal histories tell us, there was an official postal system in colonial Boston. Deputies of the English King delivered the mail. Later an enterprising Scotsman named Dunbar offered to deliver mail by horseback, for a fee, to the settlers on Long Island. As roads improved the mail was sent in bags by stagecoach to strategic crossroads and villages, and retrieved by the addressees at designated places in shops, inns and taverns.

American statesman and inventor Benjamin Franklin was appointed Deputy Postmaster General for the colonies in 1753. After the Revolution, the new American federal government regulated mail service for all the States. Jericho's first official Post Office was established two decades later on October 1, 1802, to serve the twenty or thirty families settled in the area around the Spring Pond. Linder Braner's history *The Mailman Cometh to Jericho* tells the story well.

Most Jericho families were Quaker farmers of English ancestry, but there were still a few Dutch here and there—including the first Postmaster, William Guthe. Guthe was appointed by the Postmaster General of the United States, who served under President Thomas Jefferson. Jericho's first Post Office was in part of Guthe's home (research hasn't yet revealed the home's location). Thanks to a constantly changing political climate, Guthe would be only the first of twenty-eight Postmasters to serve Jericho in the next two centuries.

Jericho Turnpike was already a fairly well developed route from New York City in Guthe's day, and continued further out to Suffolk. So as Braner notes, Jericho residents received their mail before neighboring places. Hicksville residents had to travel to Jericho to pick up their mail for the next half century, until establishing their own post office in 1855. Postal rates, in those days, were determined by the weight of the letter and the number of miles it was sent. A letter weighing less than one ounce and not going more than twenty-five miles cost six cents, while a letter on four sheets of paper traveling five hundred miles cost one dollar. The U.S. Congress issued the first postage stamps in 1847—modeled after the British system of 1840, with pre-payment not a requirement until 1855.

William Guthe stayed on the job as Jericho's first Postmaster for ten years, when Daniel Underhill, son of Adonijah and Phebe Willets Underhill, succeeded him. Local archives show he served from 1813 to 1821, and was also appointed "Pounder" and "Fence Viewer" by the Town of Oyster Bay. His Postmaster responsibilities were thus augmented by decisions on stray animals and fence repair.

Dr. Morris M. Rogers, Postmaster from 1821 to 1826, also had extra duties beyond the postal and medical: he served as Water Commissioner, Overseer of Highways and Commissioner of Schools as well. We already know Jericho's fourth Postmaster, Valentine Hicks, who served for thirteen years, 1826-39. Valentine and his father and partner Isaac had made money in ships in New York City and in 1804 Valentine married Elias and Jemima Hicks's daughter Abigail and had three daughters.

Albert G. Carll, eldest son of Dr. Selah Carll and neighbor of Elias Hicks, succeeded Valentine Hicks as Postmaster—serving just three years until followed by Jacob Ellison in 1841, whereupon Carll served again for the next eight years. Charles Willets, a descendant of Richard and Mary Washburne Willets, was appointed to the post in 1852 and in 1854 Albert Carll was named Postmaster yet again. He served for five years this time—which gave him a total of fifteen years of service.

George Tappan's Jericho General Store and Post Office, c 1859 (JPL Archives).

It was in 1859 that the Post Office finally moved out of the private home into its own space—often a small corner of a general store where it stayed, in one store or another, for the next one hundred years! (Today the Jericho Post Office has its own up-to-date quarters on Broadway, next door to the local supermarket as if echoing the past.) George Tappan, an ancestor of Jericho Cider Mill's owner, was proprietor of Jericho's first small general store. He was appointed Postmaster in 1859 and served Jericho throughout the Civil War years. Inaugurating Jericho's "general store" postal tradition, he hung a small "Post Office" sign

Everyone had to come to the Post Office to pick up their mail. . . . We got mail twice a day, in the morning and at six o'clock . . . so when the last mail was sorted everyone would be gathered around the General Store. . . . The chauffeurs would come with their large leather bags. . . . You met the whole town at six o'clock. I am probably the first "letter carrier" in Jericho. On my way [to school in the 1920s] I would drop off mail at several of the homes. . . . I got a quarter for delivering the mail for the week.

—Oral history transcript of Marty Halleran, Jericho resident, 1976

over the front door. Public notices soon began to be posted in the windows of the shop or tacked to its shutters.

Edgar Davis, the ninth Postmaster (1866-70), was a farmer and a schoolteacher at the Quaker School next to the Meeting House, and served as Justice of the Peace as well from 1867 to 1869. He owned the Davis Bottling Works located on his farm. General Store owner George Tappan was reappointed in 1870 and held office until 1886, working for a grand total of twenty-three years—making him Jericho's longest serving Postmaster. In 1872 he was appointed Constable by the Town of Oyster Bay. The Post Office was once again in his store.

After the term of the tenth Postmaster, Benjamin Smith (1886-90), the Post Office moved into a corner of a grocery store owned by Robert Seaman and Louis Van Wicklin "a bit further down street opposite the old inn" at Jericho Corners. Seaman served as Postmaster for the next four years—we know him as the great grandson of Elias Hicks. He lived to be ninety years old, and witnessed the transformation of Jericho from a rural crossroads to a suburban community when his daughter Phebe Underhill Seaman sold her property in 1952.

The twelfth Postmaster was Augustus Remsen (1894-99), who served as Justice of the Peace as well. The Post Office was now in his grocery store, which burned down in 1895, but Remsen was able to relocate the Post Office into Eugene Robbins' butcher shop nearby. In 1897, Samuel J. Underhill built a new grocery store with partners Roy Hicks and Irving Place. The Post Office was reestablished in this new store—the General Store shown in photographs of Jericho Corners—and remained there for the next sixty years in the first lengthy stay it had ever had. The building itself was repositioned, moved back a bit on its site, when the DOT straightened Jericho Turnpike in 1929.

By the turn of the century the population of Jericho had grown to more than four hundred people. James K. Hicks, the next Postmaster (1899-1915), owned a small blacksmith shop with a paint store on the upper level at the intersection of Jericho Turnpike and Oyster Bay Road (Route 106). His building burned down in 1903 and was replaced by a one-story building, and soon joined by the Halleran brothers garage and the little house next to the

It was in 1859 that the Post Office finally moved out of the private home into its own space—often a small corner of a general store where it stayed, in one store or another, for the next one hundred years!

General Store. Store owner Roy Hicks, Postmaster from 1915-20, succeeded James Hicks and ran the store. Percy A. Remsen, son of former Postmaster Augustus Remsen, became Roy's assistant and succeeded him in 1920.

It was in about 1928 that the New York State Highway Department decided to physically move Jericho Turnpike south—right through Halleran's Garage and the General Store. So land was purchased from the Jackson family and the buildings were moved "down street," southeast of the relocated Turnpike. The Post Office moved right along with them. Roy Hicks decided to retire to California so Percy took over the General Store, now called Remsen's Store, and would manage it for the next fifteen years until 1943.

Linda Braner records that Michael Freeman (1934-35) was the next postal appointee under President Franklin Delano Roosevelt and was succeeded by his daughter Catherine within a year. Catherine Freeman Trukafka was our first woman Postmaster. Jericho's population rose to more than five hundred people in 1943, and Catherine Trukafka soon took on Signe Hopp Halleran—whose brothers-in-law ran the garage—as a part-time assistant. Ten years later Mrs. Halleran, at age thirty, became the youngest female acting Postmaster in Nassau County. Her appointment was confirmed in 1954.

By the following year, when developers Green and Strow built one hundred fifty-two houses on the Phebe Underhill Seaman property as Oakwood Estates, the number of postal patrons had jumped to six hundred—but the tiny Post Office still occupied a mere ninety-eight square feet in the General Store. It now had one hundred twenty-five individual mailboxes and two service windows. One window was for mail and stamps, and the other for parcel post. The now-defined Post Office district boundaries began at the old Bostwick Polo field, two miles west toward Westbury, and two miles east to Robbins Lane, two miles north to Tappantown Lane, now Fruitledge, and one mile south to 16th Street. The district also included some of the large estates north of Jericho Turnpike.

The times were now changing rapidly. The Korean War was over, and another building boom was taking place. Marion Jackson died and a large parcel of her land south of the Turnpike east of Broadway was sold for development. Her house was saved as a landmark and moved to the grounds of Friends Academy in Locust Valley. Amazingly, another one thousand homes were added to the hamlet of Jericho, in a development called East Birchwood built on the old

Mrs. Halleran Sr at the parcel post window, 1950s
. . . The Annex, 1950s (Braner Collection, JPL Archives).

Post Office sign over the old General Store's front door, 1950s (Braner Collection, JPL Archives). . . . Mrs. Martin Halleran Sr assists her daughter-in-law Signe Hopp Halleran, postmistress, at the Post Office in the General Store (Halleran Collection, JPL Archives).

The times were now changing rapidly. The Korean War was over, and another building boom was taking place.

Post Office interior, 1950s. This tiny space, only 98 square feet, served over 600 patrons. It had 125 individual mailboxes and two service windows—one for stamps and one for parcel post (Halleran Collection, JPL Archives).

Barbara Vaughan in the Annex behind the General Store. The Post Office got overwhelmingly busy when East Birchwood was built. Solution? Open a P.O. Annex in the barn out back, to deal with the huge overflow of mail (Halleran Collection, JPL Archives). . . . Handwritten sign announces Post Office closing in the General Store, and directs patrons to the new Post Office on Broadway, c 1958 (Braner Collection, JPL Archives).

The brand new colonial brick Post Office under construction on Broadway, 1958 (Halleran Collection, JPL Archives). . . . The new Post Office is officially completed with flag flying; Waldbaum's is attached at left (Braner Collection, JPL Archives).

On October 20, 1958, for the very first time, seven mail carriers started home delivery to Jericho's eight thousand residents. William Healy was hired as the first mail carrier. . . . The formal dedication of the new Post Office took place on a cold and snowy day on Sunday, April 12, 1959, at 2 pm.

New Post Office Dedication on a snowy day, April 12, 1959, complete with the Mitchel Army Air Force Band, politicians, community leaders, postal officials and Mrs. Signe Hopp Halleran, then the youngest Postmistress in Nassau County (Halleran Collection, JPL Archives).

Jackson property. Jericho's population catapulted to eight thousand and the tiny Post Office was swamped with mail. More pigeonholes were built and soon the overflow had to be stored in cartons awaiting pickup. The Christmas rush now made it obvious that more help and more room were needed fast. An old garage barn in the back, nicknamed The Annex, was used to handle some of the overflowing mail.

Once the East Birchwood homes were occupied, the Princeton Park development went up west of Broadway. This was soon followed by the West Birchwood Development between the Parkway and the Expressway west of Broadway just to the south, with eight hundred or more new houses. The Long Island Expressway was extended eastward. The DOT's plans included an aluminum pedestrian bridge to be built over Jericho Turnpike near Cantiague and Brush Hollow roads. The plans also called for a cloverleaf at the intersection of Jericho Turnpike and Routes 106-107 (as mentioned, completed later in 1961) that would demolish the buildings on the four corners at the heart of old Jericho. The population growth continued unabated, but the Post Office stayed in its spot in the General Store and Annex.

The Birchwood developers, Sosnow and Schwartz, also had plans for a large shopping center with a supermarket, a bank and several stores. They agreed to include a new Post Office in their project. The red brick building was colonial in its architectural style and completed by 1958. It was a spacious twenty-five-hundred square feet with two hundred thirty-one individual mail boxes in the foyer—a big change from the ninety-eight square feet in the old General Store. A large Waldbaum's supermarket went up next to the Post Office, joined by some small shops and a bank.

On October 20, 1958, for the very first time, seven mail carriers started home delivery to Jericho's eight thousand residents. William Healy was hired as the first mail carrier in Jericho. Bill was a considered a good friend by the community when he retired in 1985 after twenty-seven years of service.

The formal dedication of the new Post Office took place on a cold and snowy day on Sunday, April 12, 1959, at 2 pm. Three hundred people turned

Post Office Employees—Signe, Everal and Beatrice Halleran and others pose on a mail cart in 1958 (Halleran Collection, JPL Archives). . . . Postmistress Signe Halleran with corsage and smile, at the opening of the new Post Office, 1959 (Braner Collection, JPL Archives).

Jericho Postmasters, 1802-2009

1st	William Guthe	1802-12
2nd	Daniel Underhill	1813-21
3rd	Morris M. Rogers	1821-26
4th	Valentine Hicks	1826-39
5th	Albert G. Carll	1839-41
6th	Jacob Ellison	1841-44
	Albert G. Carll	1844-52
7th	Charles Willets	1852-54
	Albert G. Carll	1854-59
8th	George Tappan	1859-66
9th	Edgar Davis	1866-70
	George Tappan	1870-86
10th	Benjamin S. Smith	1886-90
11th	Robert Seaman	1890-94
12th	Augustus Remsen	1894-99
13th	James K. Hicks	1899-1915
14th	Roy Hicks	1915-20
15th	Percy A. Remsen	1920-34
16th	Michael Freeman	1934-35
17th	Catherine F. Trukafka	1935-53
18th	Signe Hopp Halleran	1954-72
19th	Henry A. Totter	1972-88
20th	Thomas F. DiGiacomo	1988-89
21st	Janice S. Conroy	1989-89
22nd	Edward C. Pitre	1989-90
23rd	Richard Delgado	1990-90
24th	Paul R. Pluda	1990-94
25th	Richard A. Humann	1994-99
26th	Maria Scanna	1999-2000
27th	Kenneth E. Washington	2000-04
28th	Tina Laudiero	2004-present

Thanks to a constantly changing political climate, Guthe would be only the first of twenty-eight Postmasters to serve Jericho in the next two centuries. . . .

out for the ceremony. Martin Penn, Chairman of the Jericho School Board, hosted the gala event. There were speeches by local politicians, U.S. Postal officials and the current Postmaster, Mrs. Signe Halleran. She was presented with an American flag that had once been flown over the Capitol in Washington, D.C. The Post Office building also received the blessings of Monsignor George Bittermann of St. Ignatius Loyola Roman Catholic Church in Hicksville, and Rabbi Simeon Kobrinetz of the Jericho Jewish Center. The Continental Air Command Band of Mitchel Army Air Force Base provided music for the ceremony.

Mrs. Halleran continued her dedicated work until 1972, as the Post Office grew and changed service categories from a Third-Class to a Second-Class Office serving a population of more than twelve thousand; it is now called a First-Class Associate Office of the Hicksville Sectional Center. Henry Totter was promoted from Assistant to Postmaster in 1972. He was followed by Thomas F. DiGiacomo in 1988, who in turn has had eight successors as noted in the list included here.

Postmasters come and go today without much publicity. Some retire; some go on to bigger Post Offices and more responsibility. There is less interaction between the community and the Post Office in this age of E-mail, cell phones and faxes. Evidence of this change is that in 2004, many of the local sidewalk mail drop boxes were removed from the neighborhood as no longer used enough to be cost effective.

The now forty-year-old Waldbaum's supermarket was relocated in 2005 to updated larger space south of the Expressway. The entire shopping center was rebuilt to house the brand new Whole Foods store constructed on the site with modern shops that are thriving today. The bank and our red-brick colonial-style Jericho Post Office, with its colorful two-century history, complete the shopping center. □

There were speeches by local politicians, U.S. Postal officials and the current Postmaster, Mrs. Signe Halleran. She was presented with an American flag that had once been flown over the Capitol in Washington, D.C.

A single car heads along dusty Jericho Turnpike toward the General Store at the Corners (r), 1920s (photographs courtesy Detroit Public Library, Automobile Collection, and JPL Archives).

JERICHO TURNPIKE 11

We'd stand on the corner of Jericho Turnpike and Broadway hawking bunches of lilacs through the traffic, which would be bumper to bumper, stop and go, coming back on Sunday afternoon in the summertime because Jericho Turnpike was one of the main east-west arteries.

—Oral history transcript of Jericho resident, artist, policeman and volunteer fireman Marty Halleran Jr, 1976

Native Americans on Long Island preferred to travel by canoe when they could, because it was clearly the quickest way to get from one place to the next. Those who didn't live near water created footpaths as they traveled from place to place. Soon the most heavily used paths developed into regular trails.

Jericho Turnpike is the perfect example of a road that grew from a well-defined Native American trail that began at the East River and ended in Montauk. It originated near the old Fulton Ferry in Brooklyn, and ran east for thirty miles through Jamaica to Jericho. In 1703 this popular route, now used by settlers as well, was designated by the colonial government as a King's Highway. Farmers used this road to get their produce to city markets, and peddlars used it to take their wares out to the countryside to sell. Horse and carriage or wagon was the only means of moving goods at this time, unless one had convenient access to water transport.

Long Island's turnpikes soon became a popular way of building and keeping roads in good repair. The Jamaica and Rockaway Turnpike Corporation, one of the first, laid out a fifteen-mile road between Jamaica and Rockaway in 1807. It cost an impressive $20,000. The company built the road and charged travelers a toll, or user fee, probably less than a penny a mile. The road was constructed of soil plowed into the center of the road and scraped flat, creating ditches for runoff—hence the name "highway." Stones were removed. Logs or planks were laid down where the soil was too muddy. These roads required constant maintenance and toll money enabled the company to pay for repairs—and for many years resulted in large profits for its investors.

Regular fees were set for the size of a vehicle, number of horses pulling it, number of people on it or the size of its cargo. Those out for a pleasurable trip to the seashore or countryside preferred using the turnpikes because it gave them a more comfortable ride than rough country roads. Traveling salesmen, peddlars and "journeymen"—craftsmen—as well as farmers, loggers and cattlemen were frequent users of the new turnpike.

Halleran Garage at Jericho Corners, 1920 . . . . Halleran Garage, 1920s (photographs, JPL Archives).

The Commission also planned the rerouted Turnpike to cross the Hicksville Road (Broadway) right where the General Store and Post Office, Halleran's Garage and blacksmith shop were located.

Jericho Corners, 1928, with Maltby's Jericho Garage (l) that would later become the first Jericho Firehouse. The General Store is at right (JPL Archives).

The Jericho Turnpike Company was incorporated on March 20, 1813, six years after the first fifteen-mile Jamaica–to–Rockaway stretch was completed. A twelve-mile-long toll road was now built from Queens Village to the hamlet of Jericho. The road began at the intersection of 212th Street and Hempstead Turnpike in Queens Village, and along it stood two tollbooths—one in Bellerose and a second east of the intersection of Cantiague Rock Road and Union Avenue in Jericho. Some canny farmers tried to evade the tolls by turning off the road when the tollbooth came into view and reentering it further along. They were often chased down by the toll collector and made to pay anyway!

The Jericho Turnpike Company had a quiet history for the next forty years. An 1848 map published by J. H. Colton refers to North and South Post Roads. Jericho Turnpike was listed as the Middle Post Road, and shows a toll gate on the road between the towns of Jamaica and Hempstead.

In 1852, the New York State legislature passed the Plank Road Act, and the Jericho Turnpike Company reincorporated itself into the Jericho Plank Road Company. The newly renamed company hired H. Leo Nelson & Co. to grade and line the road with wooden planks—a popular method at the time. By 1869, the Jericho Plank Road was proclaimed to be in the best condition of all the turnpikes in Queens County, which, as mentioned, then included present-day Nassau County. A few years later the Jericho and Smithtown Turnpike Company was formed, and Jericho Turnpike was officially extended eastward to the Nissequogue River near Smithtown.

But by 1887, the original Jericho Turnpike was seventy-five years old, and charges of neglect to the road between Queens Village and Floral Park were documented in Queens District Attorney records presented to a grand jury. When the company tried to extend its charter with the North Hempstead Town Supervisors in 1889, their request was turned down. The company appealed to the New York State Legislature to no avail. A Flushing newspaper announced in February 1890 that the road had been abandoned, as the directors had allowed the road to deteriorate further.

A group of stockholders now attempted to reorganize the company but the Underhills, who were among the largest stockholders, refused on the grounds that the revenue from tolls was not sufficient to keep the road in proper repair. The Jericho Turnpike Company finally voted to abandon the toll road and let it revert to local municipalities. On May 24, 1890, the tollhouse and adjoining barn were sold at auction for $58.

Within the coming year, the towns of Jamaica, Hempstead, Flushing and North Hempstead voted to "macadamize," or pave, their section of the road with gravel and tar as far as the Oyster Bay Long Island Rail Road crossing, which of course made a huge improvement to the roadway. A stretch of the Turnpike from New Hyde Park to Jericho was the scene of the early Vanderbilt Cup Races, sponsored by the famed young William K. Vanderbilt II, from 1904 to 1910.

In 1927, the New York State Highway Commission decided to remove the dangerous "Death" curve that so threatened all Turnpike drivers. The Commissioner rerouted the Turnpike to run straight just south of the Jericho Meeting House, as we see it today. Old Jericho Turnpike is still in use north of the Meeting House, just in front of the Malcolm House.

Jericho Hotel in the winter, 1950s, at the intersection of Jericho Turnpike and Routes 106-107, with Daniel Underhill house in the background (Halleran Collection, JPL Archives).

The General Store, Halleran's Garage, the Post Office, the Hobbyhorse Antique Shop, the Jericho Hotel, the Firehouse and several grand old Quaker homesteads were now demolished . . .

Jericho Corners, 1950s, with the new water tower rising over its surroundings. The General Store and Remsen's Antique shop were facing a busy road now (Halleran Collection, JPL Archives). . . . General Store interior, 1950s, with its cheerful employee ready to serve you. Notice the beef prices posted on the shelf behind him—"49 cents for sirloin" (Braner Collection, JPL Archives).

The Commission also planned the rerouted Turnpike to cross the Hicksville Road (Broadway) right where the General Store and Post Office, Halleran's Garage and blacksmith shop were located. So, George Halleran purchased some land from Mrs. Jackson, widow of Willets House owner Sidney W. Jackson. The Halleran buildings were physically picked up and moved to a location further southeast before the altered Turnpike was finished in the fall of 1929.

Today Old Jericho Turnpike is a quiet two-lane road used to reach the Jericho Meeting House, and the front entrance of the Maine Maid Inn. It runs through the heart of the Jericho Historic Preserve between the Malcolm House and Barns, and is used mostly as a mini shortcut from Route 106 to Jericho Turnpike.

About 1960, a devastating change came with further "improvements" to Jericho Turnpike. The N.Y. Department of Transportation decided to widen Broadway and build a cloverleaf over it at the intersection of the Turnpike and Routes 106 and 107. In so doing, it is widely felt, the federal agency destroyed the heart of the hamlet of Jericho. The General Store, Halleran's Garage, the Post Office, the Hobbyhorse Antique Shop, the Jericho Hotel, the Firehouse and several grand old Quaker homesteads were now demolished in the name of progress. It was truly a sad day for Jericho when this happened.

Sad day for Jericho: Jericho Corners is demolished for the new roadwork. Smoke comes from the debris of Daniel Underhill's former house, c 1959 (Braner Collection, JPL Archives). . . . Police direct traffic around Jericho Corners demolition, c 1959, with Milleridge Inn at far right (Braner Collection, JPL Archives).

Today, nearly two centuries after construction of the original twelve-mile toll road from Queens Village to the hamlet of Jericho, Jericho Turnpike/Route 25 has become one of Long Island's major east-west roads, running all the way from Queens east to Smithtown, where it changes its name to Middle Country Road and continues on to the Wading River area. □

Heading south on expanded Routes 106-107 under the cloverleaf's new Jericho Turnpike overpass, c 1962 (Braner Collection, JPL Archives).

Vanderbilt Cup Race passes through excited crowds in Jericho, right in front of Maltby's Garage, aka "Locomobile Headquarters," c 1908 (JPL Archives). . . . Old Number 16, the famous Locomobile, took part in the Race's 1954 reenactment (Halleran Collection, JPL Archives).

Jericho Turnpike's famed "Death Turn" as seen in an early post-card, 1908. Daniel Underhill house appears at right (Tollaver Collection, JPL Archives).

In 1927, the New York State Highway Commission decided to remove the dangerous "Death" curve that so threatened all Turnpike drivers.

Vanderbilt Cup Races on Jericho Turnpike, 1904-1910

As the gray dawn of Oct. 8th [1904] broke over the oil-soaked Jericho Turnpike, America was experiencing for the first time the spirited and picturesque prelude which for ten years had attended the great races of Europe. All roads leading to the grandstand and other points of vantage were choked with all manner of vehicles and excited throngs on foot. The honking of horns, the throbbing of engines, the expletives of those maneuvering horse-drawn rigs in the tangle joined the songs and laughter of those camping around roadside bonfires. The environment was charged with expectancy, with hilarious anticipation. Never before had this peaceful countryside been the scene of such tumultuous nocturnal invasion.

—*The Checkered Flag,* by Peter Helck, 1961

On Saturday, October 8, 1904, millionaire sportsman William Kissam Vanderbilt II, age twenty-six, sponsored his first automobile race on Long Island. His father had introduced automobiles to his wealthy friends on Long Island, and "Willie K" himself had raced cars in Europe for the past several years. Vanderbilt wanted to promote auto racing to test cars on an open road—which he believed would improve the quality of both American car and tire production—while also introducing his beloved sport to Long Island. He chose an almost thirty-mile stretch of public roads on which he held auto races each fall from 1904 to 1910. The races consisted of ten lengthy laps and lasted five to seven hours.

The start and finish of the 1904 Vanderbilt Cup Race was placed just west of the Westbury Meeting House on Jericho Turnpike, so the peace and quiet of the Meeting wouldn't be disturbed. W. B. Powell owned the Jericho Hotel at the northwest corner of Jericho Turnpike and Oyster Bay Road (Route 106), which became a popular spot for spectators gathered to watch drivers come around the "Death" or "Suicide Turn" on Old Jericho Turnpike en route to the finish line.

An estimated fifty thousand wildly cheering spectators lined the route, some in small grandstands set up for ticket holders. The dirt road was soaked with oil to keep the dust down. Much to their horror, local farmers and residents were banned from travel on the Turnpike for the day!

Race days were dangerous occasions. The spectators had essentially no experience with automobile races and they frequently wandered all over the road. The heavy race cars could reach speeds up to eighty miles per hour, so the public was at serious risk if they got too close to the race cars whizzing by them. The Americans drove a Pope-Toledo, a Packard, a Simplex and a Locomobile against the European Mercedes, Panhard and Fiat. All the cars had thin tires and hand-operated brakes. A mechanic rode with the driver to keep up the oil pressure, apply the brake and make repairs as needed during the race. In the second lap of the 1904 race a mechanic for the German team, Carl Mensel, was killed when the Mercedes he was riding in had a flat tire and overturned.

In the 1908 race the Locomobile, later known as "Old #16" and considered the most famous racing car in America, was driven by George Robertson and headquartered in D. F. Maltby's Jericho garage. The Locomobile won the race that year. The Vanderbilt Cup finally went to the Americans after a few failed attempts—and victories by French and German racers in prior years.

The 1910 race was the fifth and last Vanderbilt Cup Race on Long Island's public roads. The Racing Association deemed the Race too dangerous after two mechanics, Mathew Bacon and Charles Miller, died in accidents. Two drivers and quite a few spectators were also injured in that year's race.

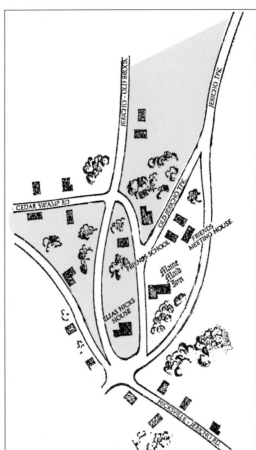

The Jericho Historic Preserve. This 20-acre property was acquired by Nassau County in 1974 to save historic homes on their original foundations—landmarks of a bygone age (JPL Archives).

Jericho Meeting House and School, c 1800, adjacent to today's Jericho Preserve. The horse barns are at left, schoolhouse at right. The Meeting house is facing away from us, toward the Burying Ground (original photograph in the Meeting House; JPL Archives).

JERICHO HISTORIC PRESERVE

12

They were historic buildings, as I mentioned. . . . But most of all it's the ambiance of the whole area, the environment that's here. The environment to the west was going to be destroyed, so we felt that at least by preserving this side of the intersection . . . that still has some feeling of a small rural community, we would be giving a permanent beneficial influence on the county's environment.

—From a speech to the Nassau County Historical Society by Ed Smits,
Nassau County Historian, 1978

The Jericho Historic Preserve is one of several unique spots on Long Island, but it is not as well known as others such as the Old Bethpage Village Restoration. Jericho was a Quaker hamlet for more than two hundred years after Robert Williams and members of his family settled here. The tiny community grew and prospered over the years, with well-maintained Quaker farms clustered around the Spring Pond at the crossroads of Jericho Turnpike and the "Hicksville–Oyster Bay Road," which is today just south of the Route 106-107 cloverleaf intersection.

In the 1920s, wealthy families such as the Phippses, Whitneys, Burrills and Mrs. W. K. Vanderbilt II bought up small farms and built large country estates in the Westbury–Jericho area. The General Store, Post Office, Jericho Hotel, barber shop, garage and a few other stores appeared at the Jericho Corners as the central hub of the hamlet.

After World War II the atmosphere of Jericho began to change, as did many places on Long Island. In the 1950s large parcels of farmland were sold to residential developers. In 1958-59, as has been noted earlier, the center of the little hamlet of Jericho was demolished by the DOT to widen the roads and to build traffic ramps in the cloverleaf pattern connecting Jericho Turnpike to Broadway.

In 1972, after so much of Old Jericho had been lost to the bulldozer, Nassau County Executive Ralph Caso announced a welcome plan to create a twenty-acre historic preserve on the north side of Jericho Turnpike—just east of Route 106 near the Jericho Meeting House—encompassing a number of historic buildings. This is a historic preserve in the true meaning of the word, as Jericho's buildings were not moved here from another location. They all still sit on their original foundations, unlike those in the more famous Old Bethpage Village Restoration, and are protected by local landmark status. The Quaker Meeting House complex nearby is listed on the New York Register of Historic Places.

To create this Preserve, Nassau County bought the twenty acres from six different owners for more than $1.5 million. The property would be operated by the Friends for Long Island's Heritage, who planned to spend about $250,000 on restoring the historic buildings and creating a special educational program in farm animal care for young children in the Malcolm House and Barn. The Friends for Long Island's Heritage used a carriage house at the Maine Maid Inn as a gift shop to raise funds to support the Preserve.

Unfortunately as the years passed the Friends for Long Island's Heritage plans were never realized and the organization was dissolved several years ago. The Malcolm House Barn was lost in 2007. Today the historic buildings look attractive and are in need of continuing maintenance. Architectural preservationists hope that the newly constituted Nassau Conservancy will continue to make vital improvements to the Preserve, as they did in 2005 to the Malcolm House, but private funding may be needed to save these buildings.

A Walk Through
The Jericho Historic Preserve

Starting from the southwestern edge of the Historic Preserve, the first home is commonly referred to as the **Ketcham-McAllister** house. Actually it was originally built by Dr. Selah S. Carll, a sixth-generation descendant of Englishman Thomas Carll (or Carle) of Hempstead, and the source of the name Carle Place. The Carlls first settled in the Huntington area in the 1700s. Years later young Dr. Selah Carll, a Quaker, decided to move to Jericho and establish his medical practice there. He purchased a few acres of land from Adonijah Underhill for $500 and had a house built for Sally, his new wife, in 1816. The Carlls eventually had ten children. In 1830, the year Elias Hicks died, Dr. Carll became one of the first members of the newly formed Queens Medical Society, and assisted in drafting the Queens County Temperance Society constitution. He is likely to have treated the Hicks family, next door, through their numerous illnesses and deaths.

Carll/Ketcham-McAllister House, built in 1816— the first house on the Preserve's southwestern edge. It was actually cut in half, c 1959, just left of the front door, to make room for the exit ramp from Jericho Turnpike down to Routes 106-107. It was later reconfigured with the left side—the conservatory—attached to the back of the house (from Family Affairs, *JPL Archives).*

Dr. Carll was also successful in real estate. He owned nineteen pieces of land including a hotel in Hempstead that he bought with Valentine Hicks. He died in 1857 and is buried in the Jericho Quaker Burying Ground on Old Jericho Turnpike. Albert G. Carll, his eldest son and a Jericho Postmaster (1844-52), and Dr. Carll's six remaining daughters inherited the property.

The house and land were auctioned to a farmer, Newberry Sprague, two years later in 1859. James Malcolm purchased the property in 1863, but soon after sold the house and part of the land to Isaac S. Ketcham,

Rebecca Sherman Ketcham, Quaker lady in traditional garb. She was small and slender, considered a "remarkably handsome old lady," and fond of saying "Keep thy own doorstep clean and it may be an example to thy neighbors." She was also known to remark "When thee is in trouble, count thy blessings" (from Family Affairs, *JPL Archives). . . . John Ketcham, son of David and Jane Seaman Ketcham, husband of Rebecca and father of Isaac Ketcham, owner of Ketcham & Jagger Cider Mill (from* Family Affairs, *JPL Archives).*

Sarah Mann Ketcham, wife of Isaac and mother of Phebe. Near the end of the Civil war after her favorite brother Captain Mann was killed, Sarah traveled to Virginia and served as a hospital nurse until peace was declared. . . . Isaac Townsend Ketcham, father of Phebe Ketcham McAllister (from Family Affairs, *JPL Archives).*

Phebe Ketcham McAllister in formal attire. She was the last owner of the Carll/Ketcham McAllister house before its purchase for the Jericho Preserve, and is the author of Family Affairs or Go To Jericho *(JPL Archives).*

who owned the Ketcham & Jagger Cider Mill. The Ketchams had been living further east on Jericho Turnpike in the farmhouse referred to in recent press as the Underhill Farm or Jericho Horse Farm, before it burned down. A generation later the Ketchams' daughter Phebe inherited the Carll house from her parents. Phebe had grown up in the house and moved to Colorado after marrying Henry McAllister. In 1939, she wrote her *Family Affairs* book about growing up in Jericho—with only two copies privately published. The originals remain in the family and fortunately a reproduction copy exists today in the Archives of the Jericho Public Library. Nassau County purchased the Ketcham–McAllister House in 1974, and rented it out to various tenants. The handsome house—which had its left side cut off and moved to the back to make room for the cloverleaf—is still being maintained as a residence.

The next house in the Preserve was built about 1740 on seventy-five acres by Jonathan and Elizabeth Seaman. It is now called the **Elias Hicks House**. The Seamans' daughter Jemima married Elias Hicks in 1771 and inherited the property from her parents. In 1832, after the deaths of Jemima and Elias, their sons-in-law sold the house and the remaining forty acres of land to James Haviland. The property—now with only two acres of land—passed through the hands of many local people, including Samuel J. Underhill, Isaac S. Ketcham and William Jagger. The widowed Mrs. William Laurie left the house to her daughters Annie Laurie Valentine and Margaret Laurie Seaman. The last family member occupant was Anna Seaman, a great granddaughter of Elias Hicks, who lived there until selling the house in 1946. Frederick M. Selchow, Henry Willets and Lester and Janice Arstark were the successive private owners of the house; it was acquired as part of the Jericho Preserve by Nassau County in 1973.

Elias Hicks house (Linda Braner photograph, c 1950).

The Nassau County Museum's original plan for this house was to restore it and keep it as a memorial museum to Elias Hicks. This idea unfortunately has not yet come to fruition. The building stands now on less than one acre of land and is leased by a non-profit group.

The next house is called the **Cheshire House**. Mr. and Mrs. Leslie R. Cheshire built it about 1930 in the same style as the neighboring homes. When Mrs. Cheshire was interviewed in 1974 she said that her maiden name was Bayer and she had been born and raised in the Valentine Hicks house, later the Maine Maid Inn, across the road, which her family called "the Homestead." The half-acre of land on which the Cheshire House stands was originally part of the Elias Hicks House property, and was purchased from Anna Seaman on September 18, 1929. The Historic Preserve plan calls for the Cheshire House to eventually be demolished, only because it was built long after the historic buildings in the Preserve.

Across the road but not part of the Preserve is the **Valentine Hicks House** that would house the **Maine Maid Inn** restaurant. It was built between 1800 and 1810, as a residence for Dr. Timothy Tredwell, who married the widow of Jacob Seaman. Wealthy New York ship owner Valentine Hicks married Elias Hicks's daughter Abigail and in 1814 Valentine and Abigail Hicks moved out from the city and bought the Tredwell house and one acre of land for $3,550—and moved in across from her parents. After Valentine Hicks died the house was bought by Samuel J. Underhill. He died in 1867 and the house went to his daughter, Phebe Underhill Seaman. Phebe and Elias Seaman, her husband, lived there until their deaths in 1905. Their son James H. Seaman owned it until 1912 and then it was held by a succession of owners, including Margarita Phipps (ownership 1914-22), William Boyce (inventor of the automobile radiator thermometer; ownership 1922-26) and the Charles L. Bayer family (ownership 1929-

Valentine Hicks home c 1850. As mentioned, the house became Mr. and Mrs. Percy Roberts' Maine Maid Inn in early 1950s (JPL Archives).

50). In 1950, Percy L. Roberts purchased it for the new site of his Maine Maid Inn. As a restaurant the house had been added on to many times, but visitors could still make out parts of the original building. Being held in private ownership the former restaurant was not purchased by the County, and is included as a landmark in the Jericho Historic Preserve.

Also not part of the Historic Preserve is the landmarked **Jericho Meeting House** property owned by the Jericho Monthly Meeting of the Religious Society of Friends. The Quakers own and maintain the 1788 Meeting House, the "burying ground" or cemetery adjacent to it and the former 1793 **Quaker School** in which Elias Hicks taught, which is now the caretaker's cottage. Jericho is still an active Quaker Meeting and Sunday Meeting for Worship is still held there.

The balance of the Preserve is made up of the **Malcolm House** complex, which until late 2007—when the deteriorating Malcolm Barn was razed—consisted of house, barns, root cellar and several acres of meadow and pasture. The Townsend family first owned this property. In 1757, Dr. James Townsend married Mary Hicks and moved to Jericho to establish his medical practice. Dr. Townsend was elected to the first United States Congress in 1789. He never took office, as he died in May of 1790, along with four of his seven children, probably from a contagious illness such as influenza. His widow left the house to live with a married daughter in Oyster Bay.

John Jackson, a Quaker farmer and fourth generation descendant of Robert Jackson, soon purchased the Malcolm

Malcolm house, built c 1757 by Dr. James Townsend for his wife Mary Hicks. It passed down through generations of Jacksons until Phebe Tappan Jackson married James Malcolm, a Scottish immigrant and a director of the Oyster Bay Bank (photograph c 1900, JPL Archives).

property. He married Charity Tredwell in 1756. They had four children, and after her death he married Margaret Wright Townsend, with whom he had five children. John's son Obadiah, also a farmer, lost his first wife Elizabeth Wright. He married Rachel Underhill in 1804, and received the property from his father in 1816. The barn burned down that year and was rebuilt, so we know the Malcolm Barn dates back to 1816. (Its loss in December 2007 would be a tragic one for the Preserve.)

Years later William Jackson, oldest son of Obadiah and Rachel, inherited the farm and made some major additions to the main part of the house. William Jackson married Sarah Tappan, and their only child Phebe Tappan Jackson was next to inherit the farm. She married Scottish immigrant James Malcolm, who along with his farming was Town Assayer and a director of the Oyster Bay Bank. Phebe and James had four children, two boys and two girls. One girl died in infancy and the boys had no interest in farming. Sarah, the youngest, never married and stayed with her parents on the farm. She continued to live in the house until her death in 1930. Her brothers then decided to divide the property—James inherited the house and William the land. After their deaths James A. Malcolm Jr inherited the entire property in 1948.

In 1974, when Nassau County created the Historic Preserve, the western part of the Malcolm land, where the barns were located, was included. The house was to remain in the Malcolm family as long as they wished to live there. James Malcolm Jr sold the house to Nassau County in 2000 and it is now a treasured part of the Preserve.

The County's plans for the Jericho Historic Preserve have, sadly, not yet been fully realized. The recently formed Nassau Conservancy has made some recent effort to improve the conditions of one of the buildings, and we hope for continued preservation efforts. □

Malcolm barns in winter, with animals in the corral when this property served as a teaching farm for children in the 1970s. The larger barn deteriorated and was demolished in December 2007 (photograph by Alphonso Gallo, JPL Archives).

*Sheep graze on the Malcolms'
back lawn, 1950s (Braner
Collection, JPL Archives). . . .
James and JayDee Malcolm
feed their sheep, c 1960 (Abbe
Collection, JPL Archives).*

*James Malcolm Jr sold
the house to Nassau
County in 2000 and it
is now a treasured part
of the Preserve.*

*James Arthur Malcolm
(with beard) seated with a
friend, c 1890. James was
the grandfather of James
Malcolm Jr, the last owner
of the Malcolm house (glass
plate negative, Doughty
Collection, JPL Archives).*

Early education in Jericho ranged from these first gatherings of Quaker neighbors to various small schools, until the first public school would open a century later in 1870.

The Old School House.   Pub. by Roy Hicks, Jericho, N. Y.

PC 10-25   1905

Building had 3 rooms.

gift of Florence Bates Tollaver

Jericho public school class, 1898. Florence Bates sits in the front row middle. . . . A 1905 postcard shows the very first public school in Jericho on the Oyster Bay Road (Route 106). It opened in the 1870s with four separate entrances—two on one side of the building for girls and two on the other for boys (photographs, Tollaver Collection, JPL Archives).

JERICHO SCHOOLS 13

There was a public school, of sorts, and I always attended it, but many of the more favored families made other arrangements for education. The Seamans, Malcolms and some others drove two or three miles to Jericho Station [in Syosset], where there was a tiny school but a very superior teacher. Some of the others went to Amy Willets's home for instruction, and all of these later went to Friends Academy at Locust Valley. Margaret and Annie Laurie and I were the only ones who received our early education solely at the public school. I believe we knew as much as the others in the end.
—Phebe Ketcham McAllister from *Family Affairs or Go to Jericho*, 1939

Edgar Davis, my husband's grandfather, was a school teacher . . . at the only school in Jericho [c 1850], which was on the grounds of the Friends Meeting House.
—Oral history transcript of Mary Davis (Mrs. Francis Davis), Jericho resident, 1975

The Quaker families of early Jericho, then as now, were staunch advocates of education, but as contemporary accounts confirm, they also believed in protecting their children from worldly influences. The region's Quaker Yearly Meeting urged each locality to establish its own Quaker school. At this early time, most children were schooled at home or in small groups at a neighbor's house. Westbury Meeting, established in 1671 and its Meeting House built in 1702, was the first to offer schooling for Quaker children after 1750. Elias Hicks sent his oldest children there, four miles down the road from Jericho.

Early education in Jericho ranged from these first gatherings of Quaker neighbors to various small schools, until the first public school would open a century later in 1870. It was in 1787 that Jericho Meeting finally qualified to build its own Meeting House, opened in 1788. Construction of a schoolhouse followed five years later in 1793. The Jericho and Westbury Meetings formed the Charity Society the following year to aid and educate black children and adults. By April of 1817 the Charity Society was operating three additional schools; the classes, successful at first, lasted only till the late fall of that year.

Elias Hicks believed so strongly in the education of children that he equated it to the "salvation of our own soul." He served as a member of the Jericho Quaker School Committee for two decades starting in 1787, hiring teachers as needed and even teaching school himself when no other teacher was available. Male teachers received $250 per year, and female teachers were paid $200. The thirty-five pupils paid six pence a day for tuition.

Schooling was considered very serious and the pupils were on their best behavior. Quaker textbooks were used to promote piety. Art, music, theatrical plays and the reading of fiction were not allowed. The Quaker School was active for just over seventy-five years, to 1870, and after that most Jericho children attended the new public school on the Oyster Bay Road. Today the old Quaker school building is used as a residence for the caretaker of the Jericho Meeting House property.

In the classrooms, a cast-iron stove was surrounded on three sides by long wooden benches used for lessons on the coldest days.

About 1830, Solomon Jackson established a small private school on Brush Hollow Road for his children and a few other Quaker children. Newberry Sprague, who had purchased Dr. Carll's house, was the school teacher there. Little else is known thus far about the school or Mr. Sprague.

In 1878 a public school called the Jericho Station School opened in Syosset. It had a reportedly excellent teacher, Miss Mary J. Byington, who taught all the usual lessons as well as French, Latin, Algebra, Geometry and Greek. The school was two or three miles east of Jericho on the north side of the Turnpike, just west of the railroad bridge crossing. It was outside Jericho's official school district, so a small fee was charged for Jericho pupils who had a long walk twice a day, if they couldn't get a ride.

Personal recollections by Jericho resident Carrie Hicks and others offer excellent insights into the beginnings of Jericho's public school system. Around 1870, a two-room public school was built on the west side of the Oyster Bay Road (Route 106). School records show that until 1895 the sole trustee for this school was Samuel J. Underhill. A fence across the front of the property had two gates, one for boys and one for girls. The building was shaped like the letter T with four entries into two rooms. Like the gates in the fence, north entries were for the girls, and south entries were for the boys. The leg of the T was the primary room and had a porch running across the front. There was a window between the two entries, and students stored coats, hats and dinner pails in the alcove formed by the doors.

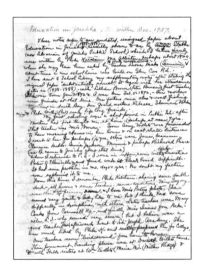

Page from Jericho school reminiscences attributed by Carrie Hicks to Phebe Ketcham McAllister, c 1900 (Esther Hicks Emory Collection, JPL Archives).

In the classrooms, a cast-iron stove was surrounded on three sides by long wooden benches used for lessons on the coldest days. Five or six rows of desks faced the teacher's platform. Blackboards hung on the walls between the windows, and sliding doors with more blackboards behind the teachers' desks divided the two rooms. Pupils had to share the few available textbooks. Lessons were learned "by heart" and recited back verbatim. When a child was deemed smart enough, or too large to fit in the primary room's desks, it was time for promotion to the big room.

Because many older children, especially the boys, were needed at home for farm chores, some older children didn't usually start school until October. Their studies included geography, grammar, arithmetic (including "mental arithmetic" done without pencil and slate), American and English history and later algebra and composition. Most work was done in school and the pupils weren't excused until four o'clock, with some facing a long walk home. Carrie Hicks records that the only entertainment for the school children was the occasional Friday afternoon "speakings," when the doors between the two classrooms were opened and an honored student would recite poems or dialogues.

Some teachers were good, Carrie notes, and others not so good, but none stayed on the job for more than a few years. The school later acquired a highly qualified Quaker teacher and many of the local Quaker children, among them the Underhills, Malcolms, Jacksons and Robbins, now started to attend the public school. These children may have previously attended another private school in the home of Miss Amy Willets between 1880 and 1885. Some of these children were apparently sent straight on to college, so education must have been on a pretty high level in all of these schools. However, most went first to private boarding schools.

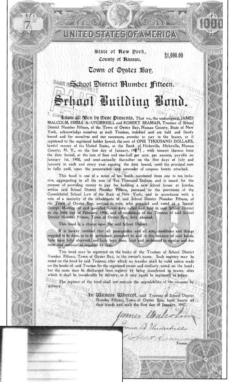

A new public school building, which construction records show cost $9,145.60, was erected in 1906-07 on a knoll just north of Jericho Turnpike on Cedar Swamp Road (Route 107). Trustees James Malcolm, Emma Underhill and Robert Seaman raised money to build the school by selling ten $1,000 bonds at

Jericho public school class, 1908. Alice Underhill is in front row, left (Abbe Collection, JPL Archives). . . . At top right, the original $1,000 School Bond—signed by Emma Underhill, James Malcolm and Robert Seaman on Jan. 1, 1907 (Burt Titus Collection, JPL Archives).

Jericho public school class, 1910. Florence Bates (Tollaver) is in center row (third from l) (Tollaver Collection, JPL Archives).

4-1/2 percent interest at the Bank of Hicksville. A copy of the 1906-07 Bond exists in the Jericho Public Library archives.

This second public school was a large two-story wooden frame building with a spacious front entrance that was seldom used. Separate boys and girls entrances on either side of the building led to four classrooms—two upstairs and two down. The two upstairs rooms had sliding doors that could be opened to make one main room for assemblies. An outside water tank supplied drinking water. Toilets were outside as well, one side for the boys and one side for the girls; teachers later got their own private toilet.

Pupils, about ten per grade, ranged in age from kindergarten to eighth grade and were taught by four teachers. The school had a full basement, where a coal furnace supplied heat for the building and served as play space for the children in bad weather during their recess period. In her oral history interview of 1976, Phebe Underhill Smith tells tales of sliding down the coal piles!

I went for a little while to the very old school [in Jericho, c 1904, on Route 106], but I don't remember too much about that. The school I went to for eight years [on Cedar Swamp Road, c 1910] had four rooms. The two on the top floor were divided by sliding doors. When we had assembly they would open the doors and make the two rooms into one big auditorium.

—Oral history transcript of Alice Underhill Mitchell, Jericho resident,
teacher and Clerk of the Jericho Monthly Meeting, February 14, 1975

Second Jericho public school, 1925, grades 4 and 5. Margaret Hartigan, then a student, is in front row (Hartigan–Wolf Collection, JPL Archives). . . . The second Jericho public school, flag flying and horseman riding by. This four-room schoolhouse was built on Cedar Swamp Road (Route 107) about 1907 (1929 Korten postcard, JPL Archives).

JPS school buses and drivers c 1939 (from l): Ted Metzger, Bud Hamilton and Martin Halleran Sr, who owned the Halleran garage with his brothers. . . . Students seated in orderly fashion on the lawn of the second JPS, c 1930 (photographs, Hartigan–Wolf Collection, JPL Archives).

When World War I ended on November 11, 1918, Carrie Hicks writes, the "concerned" school children of Jericho raised money to "adopt" a French war orphan in 1919 and 1920. Regrettably, little else is recorded about this generous gesture.

Carrie Hicks tells us that in 1926, a one-story addition was added to the north side of the building at a cost of $14,820, and a World War Memorial stone with a bronze tablet dedicated to Samuel J. Underhill was placed in front of the school.

A typical day at the 1906 public school began with a song and a reading from the Bible. Lessons were about the same as before, but now the boys were offered woodworking, and the girls cooking and sewing. Art, music and physical education were provided by

JPS student Margaret Hartigan became a teacher at the third Jericho public school. These were her pupils, grades 2 and 3, in spring 1940. . . . Students balance atop white post and rail fence of Jericho's third public school, constructed in brick in 1938, just behind the 1907 wooden frame school on Cedar Swamp Road. The older school had been condemned by NY State for lack of fire escapes (photographs, Hartigan–Wolf Collection, JPL Archives).

visiting teachers. Discipline was not a problem, for most of the children were happy to be in school and were thus well behaved.

It was in about 1920 that the Jericho School District combined with the Wheatley School District, and in 1931 became a Union Free School District with five members on the Board of Education. In the late 1930s this second Jericho Public School building—now more than three decades old—was condemned by New York State as a firetrap; the wooden frame building had no fire escapes. On December 19, 1939, the cornerstone was laid for the ultimate in new school buildings built directly behind the old frame schoolhouse, which was then demolished. This new eight-room, one-story school was colonial in style, red brick with white trim. The new elementary school, referred to as the Cedar Swamp School, was dedicated with a grand ceremony on October 18, 1940.

For many years Jericho pupils, upon graduation, attended high school in Hicksville or Westbury, or went off to private schools such as Friends Academy. In 1945 there were one hundred students enrolled in the Cedar Swamp School. But in just six years, by 1951, enrollment had nearly doubled. The Board of Trustees called in evaluation experts from Columbia Teachers College. An addition to the school was built on their advice.

Jericho's population continued to grow. In 1953-54 plans went forward to build a new elementary school, the Robert Seaman School. It was a ten-room school situated on fifteen acres at 135 Leahy Street, west of Broadway and north of the Northern State Parkway. Robert Seaman's family was, as noted, one of the founding Quaker families of Jericho. He had served as a school trustee for many years and was one of the guarantors of the first school bond. He was almost ninety years old when he was invited to the dedication of the new elementary school named in his honor and built on part of his former property.

The population of Jericho continued to grow as more developments were built. The Robert Seaman School was expanded. Plans were developed to build a third elementary school in East Birchwood, named in honor of George A. Jackson, who had served as treasurer for the first Board of Education in 1939. The school, on Maytime Drive, was built in 1957.

George A. Jackson, son of Ancel Titus Jackson and grandson of local Quaker Solomon Seaman Jackson, was born about 1880. A small, well-dressed, dapper man and avid horseman, George worked for the Fifth Avenue Bank in New York City. He never married but lived with his widowed sister Annie and niece Marion Jackson in the c 1868 family home on Broadway—the place later designated a historic landmark in 1983 and moved seven years later to the grounds of Friends Academy in Locust Valley. Today a plaque in his honor graces the front hall of Jericho High School, the next school to be built in Jericho.

In 1956, Hicksville announced it could no longer accept any secondary students from Jericho. Jericho had to make plans for a high school of its own. A ninth grade was started the following fall in part of the Robert Seaman School, and conversion of the Cedar Swamp Elementary School to a high school was completed within the next three years. A superintendent of schools was hired. Jericho High School now had forty-two rooms on fifteen acres at a cost of $3,600,000. Seven more classrooms were also added to the George A. Jackson School on Maytime Drive.

A fourth elementary school, the Robert Williams Elementary School, had been completed in January of 1960. It had sixteen rooms and cost close to $1,000,000. The Cantiague School, a fifth elementary school, built at a cost of $1,500,000, opened in 1962 to serve the West Birchwood development. But in 1977, the fifteen-year-old Robert Williams Elementary School closed its doors because of a dramatic drop in enrollment—an island-wide trend that is strongly reversing itself in recent years. The property was leased and now has a new educational role as the Solomon Schechter School, a private Conservative Hebrew school.

In 2002, another expansion and renovation of the Jericho Public High School was completed. It has been named one of the top high schools in America in the annual issue of *Newsweek* magazine that ranks public schools. □

The third Jericho public school, which was added on to and converted to a high school in the late 1950s to accommodate the growing number of older children. A new entrance with a graceful traffic circle now welcomes students (Braner Collection, JPL Archives).

Robert Seaman Public Elementary School (1954), seen here c 1972 (Braner Collection, JPL Archives).

George A. Jackson Public Elementary School (1957), seen here c 1972 (Braner Collection, JPL Archives).

In 1956, Hicksville announced it could no longer accept any secondary students from Jericho. . . .

Above: Robert Williams Public Elementary School (1960) is today the Solomon Schecter Hebrew Day School (Engel Collection, JPL Archives). . . . Cantiague Public Elementary School (1961 photograph; Engel Collection, JPL Archives).

As time passed, after enough serious fires,
several concerned citizens decided to organize a
Volunteer Fire Department for Jericho.

First fire truck "with some of the boys," 1940
(Stewart Collection, JPL Archives). . . . Jericho Fire
Department shield (JPL Archives).

JERICHO
FIRE DEPARTMENT 14

My father and Frank Tappan, and other men in the community, went around getting up a petition to start a Fire Department in Jericho. The petition was granted. This was 1931. They took over the gas station next to the Jericho Inn, which was owned at that time by a man named Curth. The community bought the building from him. . . . The first fire truck was a vehicle donated by Mrs. Burrill. . . . It was a car where they cut down the back of it and made it into a hose truck.

—Oral history transcript by Marty Halleran,
Jericho resident and Fire Department member

Before 1930 the hamlet of Jericho, comprising mostly farmland and large estates, hadn't much need of a Fire Department. When small fires broke out a call was put into the Halleran's Garage and the brothers Lott, George and Marty would run to the scene to help put out the fire, assisted by other men in the vicinity. Serious fires were called in to the Hicksville Fire Department.

As time passed, after enough serious fires, several concerned citizens decided to organize a Volunteer Fire Department for Jericho. On March 23, 1933, the Halleran brothers, Daniel Underhill, Frank Tappan, Percy Remsen, Jack Robinson, George Jackson, William and Arthur Malcolm, Frank Borley, Ray Broome and others met in the old feed store to get a plan formulated.

They collected enough money to purchase an old garage, then owned by Frank Curth, on the northwest corner of Jericho Turnpike at Oyster Bay Road (Route 106) for their first Firehouse. This garage had a machine shop out back where Curth did engine and parts repair work for aviators flying from the private airfield just south of town. The building, it was believed, dated back to 1883—but was in good condition with living quarters and a barbershop upstairs.

Ray Broome was elected the first Fire Chief in 1933, to be in charge of the Firehouse and the actual firefighting. Ernie Page was hired as a live-in custodian and dispatcher. The first Fire Commissioners in charge of the Jericho Fire District were Frank Borley, Percy Remsen, James Hewlett, Frank Humphreys and Alex Robertson. The first roll call was answered by almost fifty men.

The "Vamps" (Voluntary Association of Manual Pumpers) attended the Nassau County Fire School in April 1934, to get their training. The first fire they were called upon to

The Jericho Fire Department's first Firehouse, which had been the old Maltby's Garage—the Locomobile Headquarters in the 1900s during the Vanderbilt Cup Races era. In 1933 it was purchased from local resident Frank Curth, and the garage, blacksmith shop and barbershop upstairs were transformed for the newly created Jericho Volunteer Fire Department (Halleran Collection, JPL archives).

extinguish was a gasoline truck that had crashed and was burning on Oyster Bay Road. Mrs. Middleton S. Burrill, a wealthy widow living nearby (the Burrill estate is now the Meadowbrook Country Club), had donated her old 1910 Crane Simplex open touring car limousine that the men converted into a hose truck. It soon proved to be inadequate for the needs of the new Fire Department, so they raised money to purchase a second-hand 1932 Seagrave hook and ladder fire engine with a more effective six-hundred-fifty-gallon capacity.

The 1933 Firehouse, with its central location and volunteer spirit, evolved into a sort of community center. Square dances, block parties complete with goat cart and pony rides, and cookouts entertained the local residents. Memorial Day and Labor Day celebrations and parades always ended up with a cookout at the Firehouse. At Christmastime the Fire Department sponsored the School District's Christmas celebration. Martin Halleran Sr was usually the one who played Santa Claus and gave out candy and oranges to the children after a festive musical program. The event was considered a great treat and enjoyed by young and old alike.

The Department celebrated twenty-five years of service, and successfully combating many, many fires, by dedicating a brand new Firehouse on Broadway on October 25, 1958.

The larger building housed five pieces of equipment: a ladder truck, a floodlight truck, one fifteen-hundred-gallon pumper and two seven-hundred-fifty-gallon capacity high pressure pumpers equipped with two-way radios—all considered the latest in modern technology. The new Firehouse had a central alarm and was manned twenty-four hours a day by licensed operators.

A substation was built later on Cantiague Rock Road to house two more engines and a rescue truck. Today the Jericho Fire Department includes rescue personnel, both male and female, who are trained Emergency Medical Technicians (EMTs). The volunteers are equipped with individual pagers, and are also expected to respond to the audible alarm system. There are two Deputy Fire Chiefs, in addition to the head Fire Chief, and several Fire Inspectors assigned to check the community for fire violations. Eight trucks in the main Firehouse are used by one hundred volunteer firefighters plus twenty junior firefighters.

The 1958 Firehouse is of colonial-style architecture, built in red brick. Three flagpoles stand in front of the building, flying an American flag, a New York State flag and the Jericho Fire Department flag.

The Jericho Fire Department is constantly growing, improving and looking to expand its capabilities for fire prevention and firefighting. An ultramodern new Firehouse annex was built across the street in 2007.

Sam Toscano, the last of the original Jericho firefighters, died in 2006. Today, the firefighters respond to more than fifty alarms every month of every year, in their nearly seventy-five years of service. □

First fire truck—with Marty Halleran at the wheel c 1939. Mrs. Middleton Burrill donated her old Simplex motor car, for conversion to a hose truck (Stewart Collection, JPL Archives).

Jericho Fire Chiefs, 1933-2009

Ray Broome	1933-34
Frank Tappan	1934-37
Frank Humphreys	1937-38
William MacDonald	1938-44
Maynard Chittenden	1944-47
Anthony Sidorski	1947-49
Pat Mille	1949-50
Anthony Sidorski	1950-51
Rene Manfroy	1951-57
Ralph Fielitz	1957-59
Alan Munro	1959-61
Paul Kardel	1961-63
Joseph Mayz	1963-64
Neil Murphy	1964-66
Vito Nastasi	1966-68
Eugene Marmann	1968-69
Joseph Grillo	1969-71
Arthur Kroll	1971-73
Robert Lubcker	1973-75
William Mansberger	1975-79
Lawrence Bachteler Jr.	1979-81
Lawrence Bachteler Sr.	1982-84
Robert Zederbaum	1984-85
Douglas G. Heron	1985-87
Richard Schiraldi	1987-89
David J. Marmann	1989-90
Douglas G. Heron	1990-91
Robert T. Hally	1992-93
Douglas Heron	1994-95
Joseph J. Grillo Jr.	1996
Robert J. Kaplan	1997
Michael J. Milner	1997
Richard Schiraldi	1998-99
David Ginzburg	2000-01
John E. Lottes	2002-03
Richard G. Sandiford Jr	2004-05
Richard Schiraldi	2006-08
Glenn Gilberg	2009-present

The first Firehouse, shown in 1954 on the NW corner of Jericho Turnpike and Routes 106/107 in the center of Jericho, diagonally across from the Halleran Garage (Halleran Collection, JPL archives).

They collected enough money to purchase an old garage, then owned by Frank Curth, on the northwest corner of Jericho Turnpike at Oyster Bay Road (Route 106) for their first Firehouse.

First Firehouse, just north of the Jericho Hotel c 1950 (Halleran Collection, JPL archives).

Jericho's Volunteer Fire Department, 1939. Captain Gotthelf Lubek (white hat, ctr) stands with Cider Mill owner John Zulkofske (on his l) and former chief Frank Humphreys, whose son Bill stands in the back row with Lott Halleran, John Doughty, Harry Stewart Sr and Harry Stewart Jr. Public School Principal William Carter is in the middle row and the Toscano brothers Nick and Sam are in the front and back row, respectively. Sam was the last living member of the original firemen when he died in 2006 (Stewart Collection, JPL Archives).

Above: The second Firehouse (built 1958) is directly across from the shopping center on Broadway. It was built in the brick Colonial style like the Jericho Post Office, after all the Jericho Corners buildings, including the old Firehouse, were razed in the 1950s (Halleran Collection, JPL archives). . . . A new ultramodern Firehouse was built to supplement the second Firehouse across Broadway in 2007 (B. Murphy, JPL Archives).

Jericho Friends Meeting House, built in 1788 and still standing on Old Jericho Road (JPL Archives). . . . Alice Underhill Mitchell, Clerk of the Jericho Meeting for 40 years, with her sister Phebe Underhill Smith (Kathryn Abbe photograph, JPL Archives).

HOUSES OF WORSHIP 15

Because of where we live we had people come by horseback to the services.
That shook me for a while. They would tie up their horses and come in to worship.

—Oral history transcript of the Rev. Paul J. Theilo,
Pastor of All Saints Lutheran Church in Brookville, 1977

Religion has always played an important role in local life the world over. As mentioned, Jericho is one of the "Bible towns" of Long Island along with Babylon, Bethpage and Jerusalem (today Wantagh). Jericho was named after the Palestinian town in the fertile Jordan River Valley—described in the Book of Joshua as part of the Promised Land.

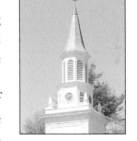

The spiritual needs of Jericho are well served by several main places of worship, listed below in the chronological order of their founding. A few are no longer here—among them the All Saints Lutheran Church, a small off-shoot of the Brookville Dutch Reformed Church and an A.M.E. Zion church—noted on a 1923 map of Jericho as "The Colored Church."

Brookville Reformed Church, 1732 (Brookville Road, Brookville)—The Dutch Reformed Church in America dates back far earlier—to the early 1600s, to a congregation in New Amsterdam. The Reformed Church evolved from the Protestant Reformation that swept Europe under the leadership of Martin Luther and John Calvin.

In 1732, members of the Protestant Dutch Congregation of Oyster Bay met at the home of local resident Jurian Haff and decided to purchase land in Wolver Hollow for a church in which the local people could worship in Dutch, their native language. Adrian Hegeman, Jacob Van Noorstrant, Barent Van Wyck and Haff raised money and purchased the land that year.

The first building, lit by a few small windows, was quite modest with a dirt floor and a few wooden benches. The congregation shared their Dutch-speaking minister with other local Dutch churches. The popular church prospered for one hundred years before a new building was built on the site in 1832. The Rev. Robert Quinn, the first full-time minister, arrived in 1835, and a parsonage was built on Northern Boulevard and Wolver Hollow Road. The Church was incorporated as the Reformed Dutch Church of Oyster Bay in 1849.

Two decades later in 1870, the Rev. J. H. Smock came over from Brookville every Sunday afternoon to preach to a large audience in the first Jericho Public School on the Oyster Bay Road (Route 106). T. B. Imlay served as superintendent of the Sabbath School.

Brookville Reformed Church, Spring 2007 (B. Murphy, JPL Archives).

When the school board no longer permitted this use of the public school, the growing congregation decided to build their own chapel in Jericho, just north of the Cider Mill, on property donated by Lewis Ficken.

The Jericho chapel was dedicated in April 1871. The Rev. M. Swick, who had by this time replaced Rev. Smock in Brookville, preached there until 1875. Theological students from a seminary in New Brunswick, New Jersey, then filled the pulpit until the Rev. H. DeVries was hired the following year, soon to be replaced by the Rev. J. A. Davis, who preached in both Brookville and Jericho. Davis found the job so exhausting, however, that he gave up preaching in Jericho. The Rev. E. Schultze was hired on a trial basis for Jericho in 1880, but left after three months and Rev. Davis had to finish out the year. The Rev. James B. Wilson was soon hired as pastor in Jericho, in the hopes that they could support a local congregation separate from Brookville, but that never came to pass and the Jericho church closed in 1881.

The Dutch Reformed Church in Brookville would prosper, however, and in 1912 add a new parsonage next to the church. A devastating fire in 1924 burned the original church to the ground. Famed architect William Adams Delano designed a new church building, dedicated in 1926 and restored and rededicated in 1991. In 1955 the church was renamed the Brookville Reformed Church. The Rev. Alan Ramirez is the current Pastor.

Jericho Meeting House, 1788 (Old Jericho Turnpike, Jericho)—As noted, the Quakers left the puritanical New England colonies after fleeing persecution in England, to seek freedom to worship as they chose in the new settlements on Long Island. In the early days under Dutch rule, members of this Religious Society of Friends could be fined, jailed, sentenced to hard labor or even flogged for espousing their Quaker beliefs. Non-Quakers could be punished or fined for merely inviting a Quaker into their homes. Finally on December 27, 1657, Flushing residents issued a document called the "Flushing Remonstrance" to the Dutch authorities, in support of their right to welcome all members of every religious persuasion to their community. Persecution and arrests continued, but tolerance finally prevailed.

In Jericho, the Quaker families living around the Spring Pond met for worship at the

*Jericho Meeting House in the 1890s, with schoolhouse (today, care-
taker's cottage) at left and low-roofed horse barn at right. Meeting
members sheltered their horses here while attending Sunday Meeting
(Doughty Collection, JPL Archives).*

*The original Quaker School, handsomely preserved, is now the home of the
Meeting House caretaker (Kathryn Abbe photograph, JPL Archives).*

*Jericho Meeting House interior,
c 1950, with wood-burning stove
that still heats the building today.
At Meeting for Worship, the
Elders sit on the "facing bench"
up the little staircase, and face the
members of Meeting (Kathryn
Abbe photograph, JPL Archives).*

home of Mary Washburne Willets (today's Milleridge Inn) as early as 1687. They traveled to nearby Westbury Monthly Meeting until 1787, when they received permission to establish a Preparative Meeting in Jericho. A gathering including Elias Hicks, William Jones, Adonijah Underhill, Edmund Willis, Fry Willis, John Willis, Thomas Willits and Jacob Willets met at the widow Seaman's home to plan the new Meeting House. It would be built on land purchased from Benjamin and William Wright, just across the road from the Spring Pond.

The cedar shingle box-like Jericho Meeting House was finished in 1788, and in traditional Meeting House style a roofed porch was added in 1818 to protect the two front doors from the weather. Until 1900, men entered one front door, and women the other. The interior of the Meeting House was also divided by a sliding partition that separated men and women during their business meetings, but was not in use during their worship. The Clerk of the Meeting runs the business meeting on the third Sunday of the month after the Meeting for Worship. A raised platform with a "facing bench" is used by the elders. To this day, two iron stoves provide heat during the cold weather.

The Quaker Burying ground, south of the Meeting House, has been in use since 1790 and today has close to four hundred graves.

The Quaker Burying Ground, south of the Meeting House, has been in use since 1790 and today has close to four hundred graves. A young member of the Jericho Meeting, for an Eagle Scout project, documented and indexed all the existing gravestones at the Burying Ground in 2002. The early wooden markers on the earliest graves had already deteriorated, and this index is the most up-to-date record.

In Jericho, Meeting for Worship is held every Sunday at 11 am and everyone is invited. The Meeting House is also open by appointment for visitors, and for special school and adult educational programs relating to Jericho history and to the abolition of slavery.

Jericho Jewish Center (Conservative), 1955 (North Broadway, Jericho)—This is the oldest and largest conservative synagogue in Jericho, founded in 1955 by forty families living in or near the Oakwood development. Charles Widlitz was the first president of the congregation and the first services were held in the American Legion Hall in Hicksville. Sunday school and Friday night services were held in members' homes. Jack Grazi was the first Rabbi and Cantor.

The Jericho Jewish Center, 1960s (JPL Archives).

In October 1955, a Sisterhood was organized, followed soon after by a Men's Club. With an increase of members, the congregation rented a house and membership grew again after the construction of the Birchwood development. Within two years, the congregation purchased land for a Temple, meeting in a vacant store in the Birchwood Shopping Center until the Temple was completed in 1960. Rabbi Stanley Steinhart succeeded Rabbi Morris Cohen as spiritual leader. A Hebrew School was instituted in 1961, and the next year Cantor Israel Goldstein reorganized the Temple Choir.

Today the Temple offers daily minyans and weekly Sabbath services along with religious holiday observances with both the adult and junior congregations. The accredited Hebrew school offers both day and evening adult education and study sessions on many religious subjects and today's issues. An active Sisterhood and Men's Club as well as a Parents' Council offer programs for the children in the congregation.

Temple Beth Torah (*Conservative*), 1960 (Cantiague Rock Road, Westbury)—Conceived of in the late 1950s in a neighborhood called Westbury Hills by a visionary group led by Joe Einbinder, Temple Beth Torah was formally established in 1960. A plot of land was soon purchased on Cantiague Rock Road, and in 1963 a permanent Temple was built. Expansions, including a social hall and classrooms, were completed in 1971. A library, new office space and expanded social hall came two decades later, and stained glass windows were added in the sanctuary in 1994. Cantor Kalman Fliegelman has been at the Temple since 1962, and Rabbi Michael Katz has been the spiritual leader since 1979. An adult choir, started in 1963, now includes both male and female voices.

Temple Beth Torah offers High Holiday Services and holds Friday evening services every week. Services are also held on Saturdays, and minyans are offered in the home during the week of Shiva if requested. Education is provided in the Hebrew School and Junior Congregation services from kindergarten through the teenage years, and in adult education courses.

Temple Beth Torah in 2007 (B. Murphy, JPL Archives).

Temple Or-Elohim in 2007 (B. Murphy, JPL Archives).

Temple Or-Elohim (*Reform*), 1957 (Tobie Lane, Jericho)—This is a modern, liberal reform temple serving the Jericho area since May of 1957. The stages of its history can be described firstly as the Nomadic years, then the Emergence, the Expansion and the Unification. The congregation had its first meeting in the "Eldorado" model home at the entrance of East Birchwood, Jericho, donated for the congregation's use by developers Sosnow and Schwartz. Rabbi Paul Levenson, a student rabbi, shared with the Temple his philosophy of Reform Judaism.

The temple changed its location several times in its early history—moving from the model home to an office in Hicksville, to two different retail storefronts, back to the model home, on to a church in East Norwich and finally to the Jericho Country Club for two years, earning it the fond nickname of "the shul by the pool." The ground was broken for a permanent new Temple, social hall and lobby in 1964. Completed and dedicated five years later in 1969, the Temple retained the original model home building as a school and office. Inspirational stained glass windows designed by artist Ami H. Shamir were added in a 1995 renovation.

Today's congregation at Temple Or-Elohim is led by Rabbi Harvey Abramowitz, Cantor Abbe Sher and their religious school Principal Jill Kaplan. The Temple also offers a Sisterhood, Men's Club, Shalom Club, Kinder Club, Social Action and Caring Community Committees as well as a choir and adult education classes, a garden arboretum and a well-stocked library. The Temple sponsors family weekend activities at several places in upstate New York in addition to their Jericho activities.

St. Paul the Apostle Roman Catholic Church, 1962 (Cedar Swamp Road, Brookville)—Bishop Walter Kellenberg established this parish in June 1962, but it had no boundaries and no church building. The Rev. Daniel J. Potterton was appointed Pastor and immediately

St. Paul the Apostle Roman Catholic Church, c 1970 (JPL Archives).

met with his new congregation, about seven hundred people, at the Jericho Jewish Center—the only place large enough to hold them all. The first services were held in the Lions Club's Bingo Hall at Mid-Island Plaza, Hicksville, on July 1, 1962. The Jericho Firehouse, the Twin Theatre in Mid-Island Shopping Plaza and the Little Theater at C.W. Post College (now Long Island University) were also used for services.

A house was acquired on Cedar Swamp Road in the fall of 1962 and became the rectory and chapel, where the first mass was celebrated in December 1962. Plans for building a church on Route 106 had to be changed because of the road widening and cloverleaf construction there. The Doane property next to the rectory was purchased in 1965, and twenty-six more acres of land were acquired from Jacob Schecter. Ground was broken for the present church on July 24, 1966. Pastors since 1962 have included the Rev. Daniel J. Potterton, the Rev. William Galloway, the Rev. Eugene F. Murphy, Msgr. Mario Costa, and, since 2001, the Rev. Robert J. Clerkin.

Today St. Paul's Church has a Confraternity program and Catholic Youth Organization program for the youth of the parish, as well as a Men's Guild and Marian Guild for the women. ☐

*In September 1971 . . . ground was finally broken
for the new Library building with a final design
by Bentel & Bentel, an architectural firm in Locust Valley
which later won an award for their design.*

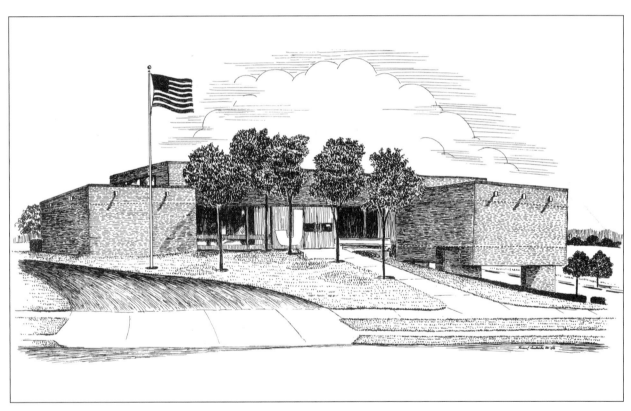

Architect's rendering of new Library, c 1972 (JPL Archives).

JERICHO PUBLIC LIBRARY 16

It was 1984 and the author Joseph Heller had a book on the best seller list. It was popular and all our copies were on reserve. A very imposing patron approached the circulation desk, and in a loud voice demanded, "Where is the copy of the book I reserved?" It being the clerk's very first day on the job, she was feeling a bit timid, and shyly asked the patron for the title of the book. The patron said "GOD KNOWS!" Red-faced, the clerk said, "I'm sorry but I have to know the title of the book." The patron repeated in a very loud voice, "GOD KNOWS!" "GOD KNOWS!" Luckily someone came to the rescue, and handed the patron a copy of Joseph Heller's best seller, God Knows.

—as told by Betty Schwartz,
Jericho Public Library Public Relations/Program Coordinator, 1982-2002

The Jericho Public Library has had an interesting history over the past four decades since founding in 1965—some moments serious, some comical, but nothing we couldn't handle. We have had our share of leaks in the roof, blackouts and systems going down. We have had visits from celebrities and student groups as well as stray birds, dogs and even a rooster! . . .

One of the most exciting, or dangerous, events happened on the morning of April 14, 2004. It was when a 1989 Mazda automobile came crashing through the brick wall on the side of the Library ten minutes before the scheduled 10 am opening to the public. The driver had lost control after being hit by another vehicle on Jericho Turnpike.

Without hitting another object, the car careened through the gas station on the corner, then crashed through a wooden fence and a guardrail, crossed a driveway, just missing the two custodians working outside, and broke through the brick wall of the Library—right into the middle of the Periodical Department. The driver stepped out of the vehicle unhurt. It was a miracle that no one was injured. The damage to the building was repaired with no trace of the accident visible today, but the memory lingers.

The handsome rooster was a multicolored adventurer from the Jericho Historic Preserve across the Turnpike. He walked in the front door a few years ago, alarmed some JPL patrons and was helped out the door with the aid of a broom.

But, let's start at the beginning of the story, with the hard work and dedication of some admirable people who got this Library built!

In 1964, a third attempt was made to establish a public library after the first two propositions were defeated in 1960 and 1961. Ruth S. Lang headed a group of one hundred twenty residents, calling themselves "The Jericho Public Library Committee," who began a door-to-door campaign. When they felt confident enough they went to the Jericho School Board and assured them there was now enough public support to put a referendum on the ballot that November. Their confidence paid off. The vote for a public library passed by almost two to one (1,535 to 789).

The State of New York granted Jericho a provisional charter on January 28, 1965, to establish a public library in the Jericho School District. A Board of Trustees was elected, with Morton Thielle as President, Hy York as Vice-President and Ruth Lang as Secretary. Florence Irving and Irving James were elected as the remaining Trustees. The Board's first job was to locate a place to build the Library and to hire a Director. On that day, Jericho became the fiftieth member of the Nassau County Library System.

Dorothy Mills was hired as the Director and Reference Librarian in May 1965 and started work in July, when the tax funds became available. A one-time federal grant matched every dollar the community spent on the purchase of books up to $50,000.

Four locations and many traffic patterns were studied for the Library site. Land on Merry Lane was "leased with an option to buy" from property owner Mac Hoffman. The Library received an additional small parcel of land from the Town of Oyster Bay, giving them a total of 22,000 square feet to build on with sufficient surrounding space. The Robert Seaman Elementary School lent basement space to Miss Mills to begin acquiring and processing books.

Franklin National Bank donated a former modular bank building they were no longer using, to use at the site until a permanent Library building could be built. This 965-square-foot trailer was moved to Merry Lane in January 1966. Volunteers, forming a group called Friends of the Library, helped process and shelve the books. Two of the volunteers—Bea Felscher and Edith Fink—prepared over four thousand new library cards for the borrowers. Residents, organizations, publishers and other libraries donated money, books and furniture.

Jericho Public Library opened in its temporary modular quarters on Saturday, February 26, 1966. Ruth Lang had been elected President of the Board, with Morton Thielle now

New Jericho Library

The Jericho Library building is moved into place at its new site at Merry Lane, south of Jericho Turnpike. The structure formerly served as banking branch headquarters for the Franklin National Bank.

LI.Press 1/6/66

Jericho Public Library started in this old trailer donated by Franklin National Bank (Long Island Press, January 6, 1966, JPL Archives).

Vice President. The staff consisted of the Director/Librarian and two part-time clerks, and a few volunteers to assist them. The trailer had no room for chairs and tables but Jericho had a Library at last!

The Board purchased the land on Merry Lane for $17,838.64, and began to interview architects for a permanent building. The firm of Ludlow and Jefferson was appointed to draw up preliminary plans and the Library applied for federal aid for the new building. In May 1967, the voters approved a $500,000 bond issue and Roz Miller was hired as a part-time Children's Librarian. New York State approved the new building plans in February of 1968.

JPL open for business in its temporary quarters. The young man on the bike is Ken Kraus, a nephew of local resident Sy Miller, who took this photograph (JPL Archives).

Trouble came in many packages—costs exceeding estimates, property issues and design problems among them. It wasn't until three years later in September 1971 that ground was finally broken for the new Library building with a final design by Bentel & Bentel, an architectural firm in Locust Valley which later won an award for their design—and are still winning awards today. The Board was very busy picking out bricks, furniture layouts and telephone systems, and unfortunately dealing with vandalism and leaking roofs. The little modular library building was soon moved to the grounds of the high school, where it could continue to function now that construction had finally begun.

An Absolute Charter had been granted on June 26, 1970. The new Library was dedicated on December 10, 1972—seven eventful years after the provisional charter. The Library Board consisted of Florence Irving as President, with Beatrice Felsher, Ruth Lang, Stephen Levine and Ernest Lopez as Trustees. Jericho Library was the first in Nassau County to be open on Sundays. The Library was now staffed by a very active Director/Librarian, two full-time Librarians, four full-time Clerks, some part-timers and a hard-working Custodian.

As the years passed the book collection continued to grow along with other services. Sheila Lesnik was hired as part-time Local History Librarian and began the Long Island Collection Archives. In 1978, Bentel & Bentel was called in again to look at space needs and to increase the Library's access to the handicapped.

Dorothy Mills retired in 1982 because of poor health. She had served ably as Librarian, Director and dynamic leader of legendary book discussions. That same year, the Library entered the computer age with its first computerized circulation system. Kenneth Weil,

Architect's rendering of the first Library, c 1970, from a printed proposal mailed to all Jericho residents (JPL Archives).

Entrance drive runs beneath the old Library, to spacious back parking lot. . . . Front of old Library, 1970s, with ivy-covered walls and hillside landscaping (Virginia Meyers, JPL Archives).

Newly completed renovation, 1989.

Circulation Desk in new Library lobby, 2008 (recent photographs, Carlos Munozospina, JPL Archives).

Children's reference desk on first floor . . .
second floor adult study space today.

"The Jericho Public Library
now has its own website that
offers instant information to the
public via the Internet . . ."

Periodical section 1990 . . .
at left, Adult Reference section.

Computer Information Center . . .
at left, computer replaced card catalogs
in November 1996.

former Director of Oyster Bay Library, was appointed Jericho Public Library Director in December.

Weil soon began work with the Board on plans to double the size of the Library building. In March 1984, voters approved a $2.5 million expansion and the firm of Lee Harris Pomeroy was hired to do the architectural plans. Their design called for excavating the ground floor to create a spacious new Children's Room, a Circulation Desk in a big new lobby, a Meeting Room and a one-hundred-fifty-seat auditorium with theater seating. Construction began in March 1985 and took two years. The Adult Section, on the second level, opened in April 1987, with two Apple and two IBM computers for the public. The Children's Room, on the new lower level, opened that September with three Apple computers.

His expansion plan up and running, Ken Weil resigned in December 1987 to become the Director of the Great Neck Libraries. Mary Donor, who had earlier worked here as a Reference Librarian from 1973-80 and was currently Director of the Floral Park Library, was hired to take his place. She handled the Library's final construction challenges and hosted the dedication of the expansion in November 1988. The Library celebrated its twenty-fifth anniversary just a year later in November 1989 and at this time bid a fond farewell to Florence Irving when she retired from the Board of Trustees after twenty-seven years of service to the community. Mary Donor led us through the arduous two-year transition from the card catalog to OPAC (Online Patron Access Catalog), completed in September 1995. Today the Library offers Internet access, online databases, reserves, interlibrary loans and a selection of programs—both educational and recreational—for adults, young adults and children.

The Meeting Room on the main floor is today often the scene of children's craft programs, adult and young adult lectures and workshops. Displays of art from local artists and groups change every month. Exercise classes, computer classes, and programs on diverse subjects such as art, history, safe driving, food and nutrition, healthcare, book discussions and current events are among the programs offered year-round for our community. The Local History Archives have a special room at the top of the stairs. The Quiet Reading Room and the Small Meeting Room share the second floor with the Administration Office, the New Book Room and the Information Center and Reference Office. The beautiful auditorium, renamed the JPL Theater, is the site of movie screenings, comedy and dramatic theater, opera and musical offerings as well as historical and topical lectures. Display cases in the Main Lobby showcase a constantly changing variety of collections. Objects from our Local History collection—as well as old Jericho Fire Department equipment, memorabilia from the Maine Maid and Milleridge Inns and the Jericho Cider Mill, and collections of model cars, dolls, pottery, wood carvings, jewelry and more—have been on display.

In 2002, John Bosco became our fourth Director, succeeded in 2007 by today's Director Barbara Kessler, formerly the Library's Head of Reference. The Jericho Public Library now has its own website that offers instant information to the public via the Internet, and together the JPL staff and Board of Trustees make every effort to serve the public with friendly efficiency. □

EPILOGUE

The hamlet of Jericho has entered the 21st century with never-ending but less dramatic changes than those of the past. New houses and commercial buildings are being built, yet we lost the Malcolm barn in the Historic Preserve early in 2007. Certain things, however, remain reassuringly constant—among them the Milleridge Inn and our famous Jericho Cider Mill—which joyfully reopens every fall. As more of the old rural charm disappears, more value is placed on the historic parts of Jericho that still remain.

In fact, Jericho never was known as a real farm community. Most families grew what they needed for their own use and only a few sold directly to markets in the city. Wicks Farm on Jericho Turnpike was the most visible. It was a commercial sod farm before it was transformed into an ocean of ship-like office buildings and sprawling parking lots. The Ketcham/Underhill farm, further east on Jericho Turnpike, was down to a few riding horses before it was sold and burned down a few years ago; luxury homes are going up on the site. The valiant battle fought by the newly created Society to Preserve Underhill was partially won when half of the open land was preserved and the rest went to new homes. To accommodate the latest increase in population, Jericho High

Today's happenings become tomorrow's history—and that is why this account is not the end of the story of historic Jericho, but the start of the next chapter. . . .

School has built a substantial addition. And in September 2007 the Jericho Volunteer Fire Department dedicated a modern new Firehouse across from the older one on Broadway.

Right next to the new Firehouse, the old Waldbaum's shopping center has been totally redone, down to a new tree-lined and landscaped parking area. Shoppers now enjoy a New-Age supermarket called Whole Foods, featuring organic foods and gourmet take-out, next to some of their remodeled favorite stores. A nearby Starbucks coffee shop is for many in the younger generation the latest hangout.

It was years ago that just north on Broadway, Marshall's replaced Channel Home Center, which had replaced the Great Eastern store back when the Jericho Atrium was built. Today, on the western end of Jericho Turnpike, a B.J.'s Wholesale Club and The Home Depot have become the new "big box" stores. B.J.'s and a new UA movie complex now thrive on the site of the old drive-in movie theater. And a grandiose new BMW car dealership now sells fine cars on the site of the old Coca Cola bottling plant on Brush Hollow Road, which in turn had once served as a school bus depot. The Westbury Music Fair—

which actually is in Jericho—is now named the Capital One Theater at Westbury.

The Jericho Public Library—which will celebrate its 45th anniversary next year—continues to receive the enthusiastic support of its community as it moves forward with new technology, programs and services. The JPL website www.jericholibrary.org has opened a portal to user-friendly databases, homework help, educational programs, local history and much more. The Library is always on the lookout for new ways to provide its patrons with the latest technology, programs and services on every level.

Jericho's community spirit is also seen in its homecoming parades, an active PTA, nine separate Civic Associations, a popular Athletic Association and our ever-vigilant Volunteer Fire Department. The list of today's active community organizations is long indeed.

Like the rest of Long Island the hamlet of Jericho will continue to change. Today's happenings become tomorrow's history—and that is why this account is not the end of the story of historic Jericho, but the start of the next chapter. . . .

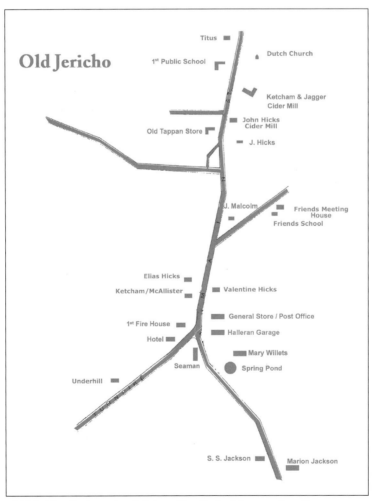

Old Jericho, "as it used to be" (graphic, Carlos Munozospina, Betsey Murphy, JPL Archives).

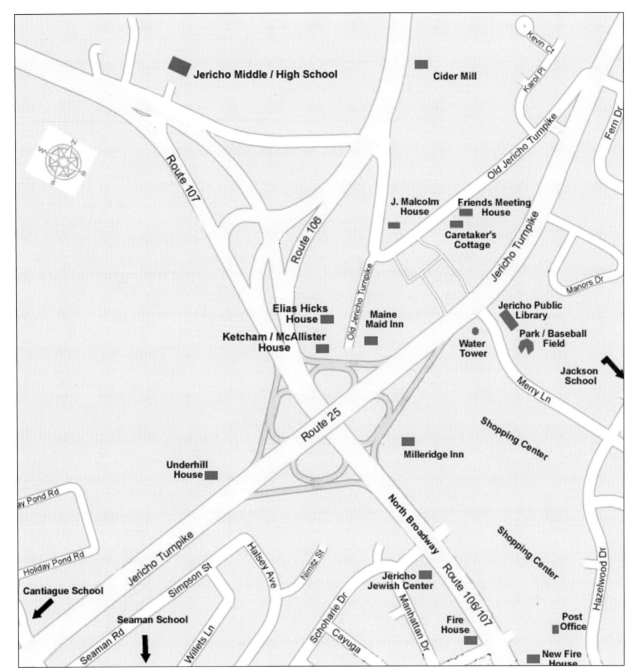

Jericho today (graphic, Carlos Munozospina, Betsey Murphy, JPL Archives).

BIBLIOGRAPHY

Bailey, Paul. *Long Island: A History of Two Great Counties, Nassau and Suffolk.* 3 Vols. New York: Lewis Historical Publishing Co., 1949.

Bailey, Paul. *Physical Long Island: Its Glacial Origin, Historic Storms, Beaches, Prairies and Archaeology.* Amityville, NY: LI Forum, 1959.

Barbour, Hugh, et al, eds. *Quaker Crosscurrents: Three Hundred Years of Friends in the New York Yearly Meetings.* Syracuse: Syracuse University Press, 1995.

Bookbinder, Bernie. *Long Island: People and Places, Past and Present.* New York: Harry N. Abrams, Inc., 1983, and 2nd edition, 1998.

Bowden, James. *History of the Society of Friends in America:* Vols. I and II. New York: Arno Press, 1972.

Braner, Linda. *The Mailman Cometh to Jericho.* East Hampton: East Hampton Star Press, 1960.

Brucia, Margaret A., and Kathryn Abbe, comp. *Jericho Friends Meeting House, 1788-1988.* [s.l.]: Algonquin Press, 1988.

Bunce, James E., and Richard Harmond, comp. *Long Island as America.* Port Washington, NY: Kennikat Press, 1977.

Bunker, Mary. *Long Island Genealogies.* Baltimore: Genealogical Publishing Co., 1976.

Deats, Edwin, comp. Harry Macy Jr. ed. *Underhill Genealogy:* Vol. V. Baltimore: Gateway Press, Inc., 1980.

DeRiggi, Mildred Murphy. "Quakerism on Long Island: The First Fifty Years, 1657-1701." Ph.D. Dissertation, SUNY Stony Brook, 1994. Ann Arbor: UMI, 2000.

Doherty, Robert W. *The Hicksite Separation; A Sociological Analysis of Religious Schism in Early Nineteenth Century America.* New Brunswick, NJ: Rutgers University Press, 1967.

Elting, John R., ed. *Military Uniforms in America.* Company of Military Historians: San Rafael, CA: Presidio Press, c 1974-1988.

Encyclopedia of New York: Vol. I. St. Clair Shores, MI: Sommerset Publishers, Inc., 1999.

Evers, Richard, and Anne, eds. *Hicksville's Story: 300 Years of History, 1648-1948. And the Tale Continues, 1948-1998.* Hicksville, NY: 350th Anniversary Steering Committee, 1998.

Forbush, Bliss. *Elias Hicks: Quaker Liberal.* New York: Columbia University Press, 1956.

Frost, J. William. *The Quaker Family in Colonial America; A portrait of the Society of Friends.* New York: St. Martin's Press, 1973.

Hastings, Hugh, ed. *Ecclesiastical Records, State of New York:* Vol. I. Albany, 1901-1916.

Helck, Peter. *The Checkered Flag.* New York: Charles Scribner's Sons, 1961.

Hicks, Elias. *Journal of the Life and Religious Labors of Elias Hicks.* 2nd ed. New York: Isaac T. Hopper, 1832.

Hinshaw, William Wade. *Encyclopedia of American Quaker Genealogy.* Vol. III. Baltimore: Genealogical Publishing Co., 1969.

History of Queens County, New York, with Illustrations, Portraits and Sketches of Prominent Families and Individuals. New York: W.W. Munsell & Co., 1882.

History of the Town of Hempstead, 1644-1969. Hempstead, NY: Town of Hempstead, 1969.

Hoff, Henry B., ed. *Genealogies of Long Island Families: from the New York Genealogical and Biographical Record.* Baltimore: Genealogical Publishing Co., 1987.

Ingle, H. Larry. *Quakers in Conflict: The Hicksite Reformation.* 2nd ed. Wallingford, PA: Pendle Hill Publications, 1998.

Kenny, Alice P. *Stubborn for Liberty: The Dutch in New York.* Syracuse, NY: Syracuse University Press, 1975.

Luke, Myron H. *Long Island in the American Revolution.* Albany: NY State American Revolution Bicentennial Commission, 1976. Reprinted in *The Roots and Heritage of Hempstead Town,* ed. Natalie A. Naylor, pp 79-126. Interlaken, NY: Heart-of-the-Lakes Publishing, 1994.

Luke, Myron H., and Robert W. Venables. *Vignettes of Hempstead Town, 1643-1800.* Hempstead, NY: Long Island Studies Institute, 1993.

Lyons, Beth. *Long Island—Then and Now:* Teacher's Edition. Boulder, CO: Graphic Learning Corp., 1989.

McAllister, Phebe Ketcham. *Family Affairs or Go To Jericho.* Special limited edition, privately published. Copy one of only two copies, 1939.

McGee, Dorothy Horton. *Sally Townsend, Patriot.* New York: Dodd, Mead & Co., 1952.

MacKay, Robert B. et al, eds. *Between Ocean and Empire: An Illustrated History of Long Island.* Northridge, CA: Windsor Publications, 1985.

Mannello, George. *Our Long Island.* 2nd ed. Malabar, FL: Robert E. Krieger Publishing Co., 1984.

Martin, Sister Mary Mass, R.S.M. "The Hicks Family as Quakers, Farmers and Entrepreneurs." Ph.D. Dissertation, St. John's University, 1976. Ann Arbor: UMI, 1994.

Mines, John Flavel. *A Tour Around New York, and My Summer Acre; being the recreations of Mr. Felix Oldboy.* New York: Harper & Brothers, 1893.

Moger, Roy W. *Roslyn, Then and Now.* Roslyn, NY: Bryant Library, 1992.

Newsday. *Long Island, Our Story:* the celebrated series. Melville, NY: *Newsday,* 1998.

Onderdonk, Jr., Henry. *Documents and Letters Intended to Illustrate the Revolutionary Incidents of Queens County; with connecting narratives, explanatory notes, and additions,* 1846. Reprinted with new index and foreword by Harriet Stryker-Rodda, CG. New Orleans, LA: Polyanthos, 1976.

Overton, Jacqueline. *Long Island's Story, 1932,* 2nd ed. with sequel: *The Rest of the Story, 1929-1961,* by Bernice. S. Marshall. Port Washington, NY: Ira J. Friedman, Inc., 1963.

Prime, Nathaniel S. *History of Long Island: From Its First Settlement by Europeans to the Year 1845, With Special Reference to Its Ecclesiastical Concerns.* New York: Robert Carter, 1845.

Ross, Peter. *History of Long Island: from its earliest settlement to the present time.* Vol. I. New York: Lewis Publishing Co., 1902.

Seaman, Mary. *The Seaman Family in America.* New York: T. A. Wright, Inc., 1928.

Seyfried, Vincent. *The Story of Queens Village.* Queens Village, NY: Centennial Association, 1974.

Shorto, Russell. *The Island at the Center of the World: the Epic Story of Dutch Manhattan and the Forgotten Colony That Shaped America.* New York: Doubleday, 2004.

Strong, John A.. *The Algonquian Peoples of Long Island from Earliest Times to 1700.* Interlaken, NY: Empire State Books, 1997.

Suffolk County Archaeological Association. *The Coastal Archaeology Reader: Selections from the New York State Archaeological Association Bulletin,* Stony Brook, NY: Suffolk County Archaeological Association, 1954-1977, 1978.

Surowiecki, James. *The Wisdom of Crowds.* New York: Doubleday, 2004.

Swaab, Alexander M. *The Long Island Story.* Phoenix, NY: Frank E. Richards, 1966.

Titus, John A. *A Saga of Two American Families, Andrews-Titus.* Baltimore: Gateway Press, Inc. 1987.

continued

Weidman, Bette S., and Linda B. Martin. *Nassau County, Long Island, in Early Photographs, 1869-1940.* New York: Dover Publications Inc., 1981.

Werner, Jr., Ben. *The Indians of Long Island, New York and Coastal Connecticut.* Port Jefferson, NY: Yorkshire Publishing Co., 1973.

Wilbur, Henry W. *The Life and Labors of Elias Hicks.* Uncatalogued rare book, Philadelphia: Friends General Conference Advancement Committee, 1910.

World Book Encyclopedia. Chicago: World Book, Inc., 2002.

ARTICLES AND PAPERS

Braner, Linda. "The Jericho Fire Department, Then and Now." *Jericho Tribune* Aug. 27, 1974: p4 and Nov. 29, 1979: p2.

Demeritt, Jr., Dwight B. "The Battle of Long Island." LI Historical Society paper from the Long Island in History series. Brooklyn: Long Island Historical Society, 1967.

Hicks, Carrie. "Education in Jericho." Handwritten essay, Dec. 1957.

Jericho Fire Department, Golden Anniversary Program 1933-1983. JPL Archives.

Lambert, Bruce, Jr. "Historic Preserve Opposed." *Newsday,* Mar. 27, 1973: p17.

Levinson, Marilyn. "George A. Jackson." *The Jackson Voice,* Dec. 1979: p3.

McAllister, Phebe Ketcham. "Jericho Public School (As I Remember It) 1872-1950." Typescript, c 1950. JPL Archives.

McQueen, Edwin. Town Clerk of Oyster Bay Address given on Robert Williams Day, Hicksville, NY, May 19, 1941. JPL Archives.

Reno, Robert. "Quaker Settlement Will Be Restored." *Newsday,* Feb. 10, 1972: p16.

Stewart, Harry. Letter to the Jericho Public Library. Received Aug. 15, 1990. JPL Archives.

"The School District and Brief History of Jericho Schools." Unsigned typescript c 1961. JPL Archives.

Weddle, Robert. "Historic Community Preserved." *Long Island Press.* Sept. 28, 1973: p23.

Weigand, Philip C. "How Advanced Were Long Island's Native Americans? A Challenge to the Traditional View." *The Long Island Historical Journal.* Fall 2004-Spring 2005: p101-118.

Winsche, Richard A. "The Jericho Historic Preserve." *Nassau County Historical Society Journal Vol. 39, 1984: 1-14.*

Wolf, Margaret Hartigan, and Leona Hicks Seaman. "Early Education in Jericho." Typescript, Dec. 19, 1939. (Date cornerstone was laid for the new Jericho Public School.) JPL Archives.

ORAL HISTORIES
Interview tapes by Sheila Lesnick, 1977
Braner, Linda
Connolly, Barbara
Doughty, George
Halleran, Marty
Hartigan Wolf, Margaret
Underhill Smith, Phebe

Internet
Ancestry.com

Interviews—
By Betsey Murphy, 1999-2006
Curth, Frank Jr.
Kroplick, Howard
Schwartz, Betty
Smits, Edward J.
Zulkofske, George

INDEX

continued

FREEPORT MEMORIAL LIBRARY